Author: Seth J. Gillespie, Ph.D.
Publisher: DBC Publishing, Virginia Beach, VA

Copyright ©   2014; 2016
                 ISBN-13: 978-0692766385 (Custom Universal)
                 ISBN-10: 0692766383

Disclaimer:

Limit of Liability / Disclaimer of Warranty: While the publisher and/or author have prepared this book to the best of their abilities, they make no representation or warranties for accuracy or completeness to the contents of the book and specifically do not make any claims to any implied warranty. No warranty may be created or extended to any specific or unique purpose by representative selling this book or written sales materials. The strategies and advice contained may not be suitable for any one reader's situation. Consult a professional for advice in any specific venue or field related to this book's topic. Neither the publisher nor the author holds any liability for any loss of profit, revenue, income, or other commercial damages, including but not limited to: special, consequential, incidental, or other damages.

The author has attempted to gather as many facts and documented information and resource to the utmost complete and truthfulness for the compilation of this book from bona-fide research, Internet sources, printed material in currently circulating and non-circulating sources, newspaper articles, personal interviews. Any dates noted were from publically available sources. If any data included (or is left out), incorrectly quoted, or attributed, it may be attributed to transcription errors or typos.

Visit the Author's Website: books.sethgillespie.com
            Author's Blog: blog.sethgillespie.com
          LinkedIn Profile: linkedin.com/in/sethgillespie
          Follow on Twitter: twitter.com/sg_phd

CORRELATIONAL STUDY OF RISK MANAGEMENT AND INFORMATION TECHNOLOGY PROJECT SUCCESS

By

Seth J. Gillespie, Ph.D.

WERNER D. GOTTWALD,

Ph.D., Faculty Mentor and Chair

GAIL FERREIRA, DM, Committee Member

PERRY HAAN, DBA, Committee Member

Barbara Butts Williams, Ph.D.,

Dean, School of Business and Technology

A Dissertation Presented in Partial Fulfillment

of the Requirements for the Degree of

Doctor of Philosophy

Capella University, January 2014

INSPIRATION

"We are here to put a dent in the universe."
— Steven J. Jobs

ABSTRACT

Many IT projects fail despite the best efforts to keep these projects within budget, schedule, and scope. Few studies have looked at the effect of project risk management tools and techniques on project success. The primary focus of this study was to examine the extent to which utilization of project risk management processes influence project success. A secondary focus of the study was to determine if utilization of project risk management processes correlates with project success more than project manager experience, certification, level of education, and project size, type, or duration.

To meet the objectives of the study, a survey instrument was developed and piloted. The final instrument was administered to a group of IT project management practitioners to assess the utilization of specific project risk management tools and techniques on a recently completed project. The answers were combined with the participants' self-reported project success as measured by end-of-project budget, schedule, and scope success metrics.

While the results of the study did not point to a specific project risk management tool or technique to predict an IT project's success, valuable insight was gained when stepping back and looking at overall factors that influence project success. When looking at these factors, the researcher found there was a statistical correlation that indicated the use of project risk management processes as a whole are a better predictor of IT project success than a project manager's experience, certification, level of education, and project size, type, or duration in the majority of success areas measured.

TABLE OF CONTENTS

LIST OF TABLES

LIST OF FIGURES

CHAPTER 1. INTRODUCTION

Introduction to the Problem

A review of the literature suggested information technology (IT) project failure rates can be attributed to ineffective execution of project risk management (Addison & Vallabh, 2002; Huff & Prybutok, 2008; Islam, 2009; Padayachee, 2002; Reich, 2007; Warkentin, Moore, Bekkering, & Johnston, 2009). While factors for IT project failure have been studied in the past, the direct relationship between specific project risk management process groups and project success, as measured by meeting cost, time, scope, and quality, is less understood (Raz, Shenhar, & Dvir, 2002). Raz et al. (2002) concluded, given the increasing importance of project success in the global economy and despite an apparent plethora of risk management tools and techniques, increased application, awareness, and research within the practice of project risk management is sorely needed.

With an estimated 50–80% of IT projects failing to meet given project objectives (Warkentin et al., 2009) and up to 20% of all IT projects ending in outright failure (Islam, 2009), the situation seems dire. However, within the last decade, researchers noted an increasing correlation between utilization of project risk management processes and project success (Addison & Vallabh, 2002). Additional authors pointed to the importance of examining project risk management processes within the context of overall project planning and success (Hillson, 2002; Kendrick, 2009; Laufer, Denker, & Shenhar, 1996; Project Management Institute [PMI], 2009; Shenhar & Dvir, 2007; Söderlund, 2004).

While de Bakker, Boonstra, and Wortmann (2009) noted a lack of data regarding how utilization of project risk management processes affect project success directly, they argued building on foundational research can inform future studies and enable deeper insight into these relationships. Future research could also build on the better known relationship between generic objectives and progress success, as is well documented within the literature (Busby & Zhang, 2008; Kerzner, 2009; Pinto & Slevin, 1988; Raz et al., 2002; Rosacker & Olson, 2008).

Background of the Study

The practice of project risk management can be traced to the standardization of project management as a profession, starting between the 1940s and 1950s (Kerzner, 2009; Shenhar & Dvir, 1996). According to Perminova, Gustafsson, and Wikström (2007), the concept of risk management traditionally has been understood as a negative event. The authors stated while most research has focused on the negative consequences of uncertainty and organization theory, recent developments proposed the expansion of project risk to include both potential positive and negative project impact. Overall, the "objectives of Project Risk Management are to increase the probability and impact of positive events, and decrease the probability and impact of negative events in the project" (PMI, 2008, p. 273).

The 1960s and 1970s proved to be formative years for project management due to the increasing size and technological complexity of projects and the dependence on more formalized project management processes (Kerzner, 2009). In the 1960s, ownership of project risk management began shifting from large departments to individual project teams in areas such as government, information systems (IS), and new product development (Kwak & Anbari, 2009). In this time period, Project Management Institute (PMI), a leading nonprofit dedicated to furthering professional project management, was formed in 1969. PMI first published *A Guide to the Project Management Body of Knowledge* (*PMBOK® Guide*) in 1987 as a white paper. The goal of the first publication was to assist in the standardization of generally accepted project management tools and practices (PMI, 2008). The work was published nine years later as a first edition, in 1996. The second edition was published in 2000, followed by the third edition in 2004, and, finally, the fourth edition in 2008 (PMI, 2008). Subsequent to the *PMBOK Guide,* PMI (2009) introduced a practice standard specializing in project risk management, which has undergone several subsequent updates, the most current titled *Practice Standard for Project Risk Management.*

In the 1970s, researchers began documenting the concept of technical project failure (de Bakker et al., 2009), which created a growing interest in project risk management that culminated during the time of major project failures, such as the NASA Challenger space shuttle disaster in 1986 (Dimitroff, Schmidt, & Bond,

2005). An additional factor in the mainstreaming of project risk management is the paradigm that considers *uncertainty* as a quantifiable and manageable variable can be controlled through the use of contingency planning and analysis (Laufer et al., 1996).

In the 1990s, advancement within the field of project risk management included better understanding of how *simultaneity* caused by human factors limits success, especially within projects that faced increasing complexity and uncertainty (Laufer et al., 1996). For example, human factors can negatively influence success when pressures of time to market (Laufer et al., 1996) and group-think combine, resulting in poorly performing teams (Dimitroff et al., 2005). In addition to human factors, technical or performance-based limiters can also affect project success (Cooke-Davies, 2002).

In addition to the best efforts to mainstream the use of project risk management principles identified in the 1990s, the 2000s presented significant growth in research, as evidenced by the extent of peer-reviewed literature produced during this period (Dimitroff et al., 2005; Flyvbjerg, 2006; Freimut, Hartkopf, Kaiser, Kontio, & Kobitzsch, 2001; Kajko-Mattsson, 2009; Kwak & Anbari, 2009; McCray, Purvis, & McCray, 2002; Perminova et al., 2007; Taylor, 2006). Due to the significant spike of peer-reviewed literature within the scope of project risk management in the 2000s, it can be argued that interest in the field was expanding. Examples of maturation of theory include the categorization of project risk in the form of taxonomies (Flyvbjerg, 2006), the concept of a quantifiable risk breakdown structure, and the publication of a significantly updated *Practice Standard for Project Risk Management* (PMI, 2009). Owing perhaps to the popularity and maturation of project risk management, PMI (2008) developed a professional certification titled the PMI Risk Management Professional (PMI–RMP)®.

Statement of the Problem

Due to reports of high IT project failure rates, it is paramount the use of project risk management tools and techniques be examined in the context of their effect on project success. While a large amount of literature has been written on generalized factors involved in project success, few studies have examined the relationship between the use of project risk management processes and actual project success as measured by project outcomes – thus, a study focused on these effects could be profound.

Purpose of the Study

The purpose of this study was to understand whether utilizing project risk management processes correlates with improved IT project success as measured by self-reported variance in planned versus actual end-of-project budget, schedule, and scope. Additionally, the use of project risk management processes could be contrasted within standardized project management process groups, including (a) planning, (b) identifying, (c) analyzing, (d) responding, and (e) controlling (Krane, Rolstadås, & Olsson, 2010; PMI, 2009). It is thought organizations involved in executing projects would be willing to change practices if confronted with evidence showing how gaps within the practice of project risk management affect project success. Due to project management practitioners' typically limited time and resources, it was suggested studying which project risk management processes affect project success the most would be particularly valuable (de Bakker et al., 2009). Variables included examination of the extent to which independent project risk management process variables (planning, identifying, qualitative, quantitative, responding, and controlling) predict each of the three dependent project success outcome variables (budget, schedule, and scope).

Rationale

In a recent survey, Kutsch and Hall (2009) found nearly one-third of project managers did not include formal project risk management within project planning activities. Given these statistics and the reports of high IT project failure rates (Huff & Prybutok, 2008), the time appears ripe to examine the relationship between risk management processes and project success. Findings from such a study may help to close the gap in the understanding and impact of this often-overlooked project management practice.

Though theories and factors affecting project success have been studied piecemeal over the years, many authors suggest opportunities exist to expand on these works with further analysis on specific project risk management practices and project success (Boehm, 1991; Busby & Zhang, 2008; Cooke-Davies, 2002; Freeman & Beale, 1992; Pinto & Slevin, 1988; Raz et al., 2002; Rosacker & Olson, 2008; Voetsch, Cioffi, & Anbari, 2004; Wallace & Keil, 2004; Ward, 1999a).

In particular, Cooke-Davies (2002) identified five of 12 factors affecting project success could be related to the effective use of project risk management processes. Despite the abundance of tools, Raz et al. (2002) expressed concern many organizations choose not to utilize project risk management methodologies. Particularly, Wallace and Keil (2004) identified that a focus on project risk management factors can positively affect project constraints such as scope, budget, and schedule.

If project success can be linked to the utilization of one or more specific risk management processes, there could be a newfound impetus for increased use of such processes within the practice of IT project management (de Bakker et al., 2009). Rosacker and Olson (2008) asserted IT project managers constantly juggle competing priorities within a limited time frame. A future study would better inform practitioners on project risk management practices that offer the highest return on investment as measured by project success metrics (Voetsch et al., 2004).

Research Questions

This study addressed the research question, To what extent does utilization of project risk management processes, project manager experience, or project type influence project success?

The following primary research question was addressed in this study:

R_1. To what extent is utilization of project risk management processes (planning, identifying, qualitative, quantitative, responding, and controlling) related to project success outcomes (budget, schedule, and scope)?

In addition, the following subsidiary research questions were asked in support of the primary research question:

R_2. What is the correlation between reported project success and project manager experience, certification, level of education, and project size, type, and duration?

R_3. Does the utilization of project risk management processes correlate with project success more than project manager experience, certification, level of education, and project size, type, or duration?

The following hypotheses were used to test the research questions:

$H_0$1. There is no correlation between utilization of project risk management processes and project success as reported by the management of project budget, schedule, or scope.

H_a1. There is a correlation between utilization of project risk management processes and project success as reported by the management of project budget, schedule, or scope.

$H_0$2. There is no correlation between reported project success and project manager experience, certification, level of education, and project size, type, and duration.

H_a2. There is a correlation between reported project success and project manager experience, certification, level of education, and project size, type, and duration.

$H_0$3. There is no correlation between the utilization of project risk management processes and project success and that of project manager experience, certification, level of education, and project size, type, or duration.

H_a3. There is a correlation between the utilization of project risk management processes and project success and that of project manager experience, certification, level of education, and project size, type, or duration.

Significance of the Study

The intent of this study was to create additional knowledge that may be generalized and disseminated to IT project managers. The end result of the study was to attempt to help organizations avoid costly mistakes and efficiently produce more successful projects. Results of this study may benefit the project management profession by validating the effectiveness of project risk management processes, which may have been a lower priority for organizations to implement or support given the extra time and cost associated with such processes. Because of the lack of focus on the utilization of risk management within IT project literature, the present study's focus may help elucidate an understanding of its value in the context of project success and inherent benefits to the organization, resulting in more efficient use of money and resources to achieve stated project requirements. The results of this study will be helpful to project managers, management, and organizations alike.

Definition of Terms

A Guide to the Project Management Body of Knowledge (PMBOK Guide). Provides a comprehensive framework and vocabulary to project managers wishing to apply standardized concepts and practices within the project management discipline. The *PMBOK Guide,* first published in 1983, is authored by PMI, a nonprofit group founded in 1969, with over 425,000 members as of 2008.

Information technology (IT). Synonymous with *information systems*; involves the use of computerized systems, hardware, software, or other technical resources, resulting in the support or creation of a tangible product or service, benefitting the public, sponsor, or other stakeholder.

Practice Standard for Project Risk Management. The *Practice Standard for Project Risk Management* is consistent with, and considered to be an extension of, the *PMBOK Guide*. Specific and generalized tools and techniques are explored and defined within a standardized set of project risk management process groups.

Project. "A temporary endeavor undertaken to create a unique product, service, or result" (PMI, 2008, p. 2). Kerzner (2009) clarified most projects have a specific objective, are bounded by a start and end date, and consume human and nonhuman resources, at the minimum. PMI (2008) further stated a project can create a product, a capability, or a specific end result or outcome.

Project management. "The application of knowledge, skills, tools, and techniques to project activities to meet the project requirements" (PMI, 2008, p. 6). Managing a project includes balancing constraints such as budget, schedule, scope, quality, and risk, to name a few. Generalized phases used within project management include project initiation, planning, execution, monitoring and control, and closure.

Project manager. "The person assigned by the performing organization to achieve the project objectives" (PMI, 2008, p. 13).

Project objectives. May vary by organization or by project, but usually include scope, schedule, budget, and quality (PMI, 2009).

Project risk. "An uncertain event or condition that, if it occurs, has a positive or negative affect on a project's objectives" (PMI, 2008, p. 438). Individual project risks can therefore be treated as either an opportunity or a threat. Risks are often categorized in two dimensions: their individual consequence and their likelihood. The riskiness of a project may include a summation of all quantified known and unknown risks.

Project risk management. The systematic process of planning, identifying, calculating, responding to, and controlling risk within a project (PMI, 2009). Project risk management is often defined by organizational practices, built on the foundation provided by a project's definition and planning, and is generally defined in a project's risk plan (Kendrick, 2009).

Project Risk Management Community of Practice. A PMI special interest group established in 2010 to provide and promote the practice of risk management within the project management profession through education, communication, and the exchange of information.

Project success factors. May vary by the specifications of an organization or stakeholder, but usually include the delivery of a project within schedule, budget, scope, and acceptance by the customer (Kerzner, 2009).

Qualitative risk analysis. Consists primarily of the identification, evaluation, and ranking of individually identified project risks. Qualitative risk analysis may be either one-time exercises or iterative; however, both provide input into the planning of risk responses and mitigation (PMI, 2009). It is acceptable to descriptively quantify individual risks with their discrete probability and impact on objectives.

Quantitative risk analysis. The process in which all project risks are considered simultaneously, usually with specialized tools that focus on the ability to predict the likelihood of meeting specified project performance targets, such as schedule and budget, when modeled (PMI, 2009). Outputs typically include quantification of contingencies needed in order to achieve specific levels of risk comfort.

Stakeholder. A person or group of people who can represent a customer, sponsor, organization, or public and who are "actively involved in the project, or whose interests may be positively or negatively affected by the execution or completion of the project" (PMI, 2008, p. 246).

Assumptions and Limitations

Assumptions

The following assumptions were made for the study:

1. As the study focused on reported metrics from IT projects, generalizations were made from an IT perspective.
2. Survey participants responded truthfully and honestly even if project outcomes were not

positive.

3. A minimal amount of project risk management knowledge as required for responding to and answering questions.

4. Individuals responding to the survey questions did so truthfully and in a qualified way in speaking to the metrics provided.

5. There was an adequate number of survey participants necessary to produce statistically significant results.

Limitations

The following limitations were acknowledged for this study:

1. It is recognized many factors can be used to measure project success (Cooke-Davies, 2002; Freeman & Beale, 1992); however, budget, schedule, and scope metrics were primarily used as success measures in the survey for this study.

2. While there is more than one project risk management practice standard, a focus on PMI's (2009) published risk management process

groups was used as a baseline of comparison in the study.

3. Study participants were sampled from a diverse subset of education, employment, and experience backgrounds; therefore, findings of this study may not be fully generalizable to all IT industry projects.

4. The survey instrument (see Appendix) developed for this study was vetted by a small, yet qualified group of subject matter experts and thus may not represent a full diversity of opinions.

5. Survey participant skill level or experience may have affected the way questions are answered.

6. Since three success scores were calculated for each survey, a combination of success and nonsuccess factors were recorded as a delimiting factor.

Nature of the Study

A quantitative research approach was used to determine if there is a relationship between use of project risk management processes and project success as measured by variance between planned and actual budget, schedule, and scope. Additionally, the study examined if the relationship between demographics and project success is stronger than the relationship of the use of project risk management processes and project success. This conceptual framework and interrelationship are illustrated in Figure 1.

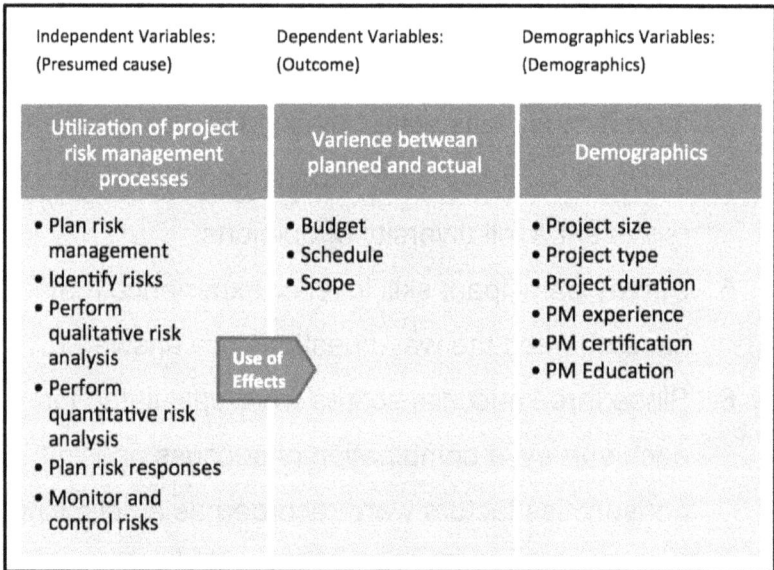

Independent Variables: (Presumed cause)	Dependent Variables: (Outcome)	Demographics Variables: (Demographics)
Utilization of project risk management processes	Varience between planned and actual	Demographics
• Plan risk management • Identify risks • Perform qualitative risk analysis • Perform quantitative risk analysis • Plan risk responses • Monitor and control risks	• Budget • Schedule • Scope	• Project size • Project type • Project duration • PM experience • PM certification • PM Education

Figure 1. Conceptual framework and interrelationship.

Organization of the Remainder of the Study

Chapter 2 provides a comprehensive literature review on the topic of project risk management, its theoretical framework, and an analysis of the process used in the study. Chapter 3 provides a review of the quantitative research design, including discussion of the population and sample, setting, instruments, data collection procedures, data analysis along with statistical analyses, validity and reliability, and ethical considerations. Chapter 4 provides a description of the population and sample, a summary of results, details of analysis, and results. Chapter 5 includes a discussion of the results, implications of the study results, limitations, recommendations for further research, and a conclusion.

CHAPTER 2. LITERATURE REVIEW

Introduction

The literature reviewed for this study reflects academic research within several closely related disciplines of risk management theory and project management, as framed by several prominent authors (Hillson, 2002; Kendrick, 2009; Laufer et al., 1996; PMI, 2009; Shenhar & Dvir, 2007; Söderlund, 2004). These works offered a defining and authoritative means by which to analyze the field at large. For example, Hillson (2002) contended risk management theory could provide a basis for "offering a structured approach to managing the inevitable uncertainty in projects" (p. 235). Along the same line, PMI (2009) argued project management theory suggests the creation of project risk management objectives are designed to "increase the probability and impact of positive events, and decrease the probability and impact of negative events" (p. 4). Project risk management theory could be seen to recast the system of categories used to approach project success, and accommodates the understanding of features integral to project success otherwise left unnoticed. This shift in practice seems to have created a paradigm change within the contemporary world of business and a move toward more thorough development and integration of risk management theory.

Theoretical Framework

Laufer et al. (1996) posited a new paradigm arising in project management related to complexity that represents an evolutionary change in principles and attitudes when it comes to complex projects undertaken within uncertain conditions. The central theory can be understood in the context of now moving quickly from *concept* to *facility*, versus the traditional approach of moving from *concept* to *definition*, to *execution* (Laufer et al., 1996). Figure 2 shows a clear shift from the old paradigm of overreacting to the what, to the more rapid execution and evolution to the how. Laufer's certainty matrix may help explain the shift in project risk management theory cited in the literature and the prevalence of practical use in actual projects.

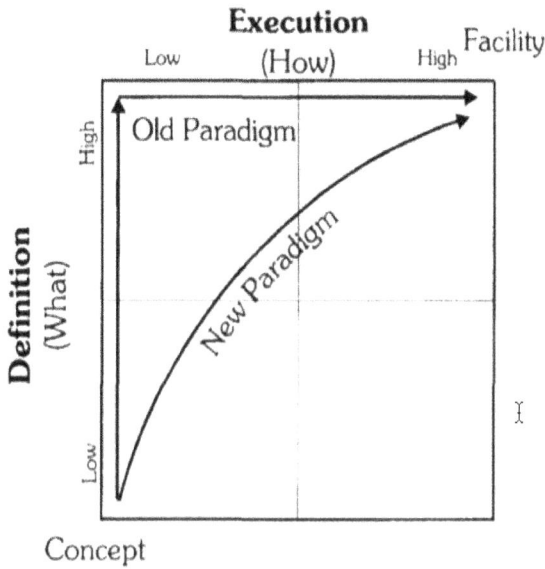

Figure 2. Certainty matrix.[1]

In addition, the evolution of models of project management (see Table 1) represent a noted shift from *control* to *integration*, to *flexibility*, and ultimately to *dynamism*.

---

[1] *From "Simultaneous Management: The Key to Excellence in Capital Projects" by A. Laufer, G. R. Denker, and A. J. Shenhar, 1996, International Journal of Project Management, 14(4), p. 190. Copyright 1996 by Elsevier. Reprinted with permission.*

Table 1. Evolution of Models of Project Management.[2]

Central concept	Era of model	Dominant project character-istics	Main thrust	Meta-phor	Means
Schedul-ing (control)	1960s	Simple, certain	Coordinat-ing	Schedul-ing regional flights in an airline	Information technology, planning specialists
Team-work (integra-tion)	1970s	Complex, uncertain	Coopera-tion between participant s	Conduct-ing a symphon y orchestra	Process facilitation, definition of roles
Reducing un-certainty (flexi-bility)	1980s	Complex, uncertain	Making stable decisions	Exploring an unknown country	Search for information, selective redundancy
Simul-taneity (dyna-mism)	1990s	Complex, uncertain , quick	Orchestrat-ing contend-ing demands	Directing a three-ring circus contin-uously switching acts based on the crowd's re-sponse	Experience, responsivene ss and adaptability

Linking project risk management to this model, and the seeming paradox of Laufer's certainty matrix predicting increasingly rapid decision making, it is clear

[2] From "Simultaneous Management: The Key to Excellence in Capital Projects" by A. Laufer, G. R. Denker, and A. J. Shenhar, 1996, *International Journal of Project Management, 14*(4), p. 190. Copyright 1996 by Elsevier. Reprinted with permission.

responsiveness and adaptability will have an ever-increasing role in project risk management.

Shifts in Practice and the Need for Risk Management

The past half century has seen a shift in business practices resulting in increased complexity in projects and implying the need for a system of categories that judge projects in terms that place a premium on risk analysis (Laufer et al., 1996). Kendrick (2009) stated, "All projects involve risk" (p. 1); *risk* is theoretically described best as a predicted event's consequence multiplied by its likelihood. Furthermore, Laufer et al. (1996) observed a link between simultaneous management and risk management theory that resulted in the increasing importance and applicability to projects in today's era as opposed to the 1950s, 1960s, and 1970s. IT projects, for example, exemplified a paradigm shift toward increasingly sophisticated needs for project management. For example, Kendrick, citing the Panama Canal project, argued paradigms have shifted from simple and certain execution of projects to the orchestration of complex yet flexible interdependent activities possessing high degrees of uncertainty.

The evolution of project management, as shown by the research, calls for the inclusion of a direct approach to risk management. Shenhar and Dvir (2007), like Laufer et al. (1996), linked uncertainty and risk management with simultaneous management theory. This linkage proposed an evolution within the field of project management, mainly due to the increase of complex projects, may help to inform future research studies that aim to synthesize theory with practice. Additionally, Söderlund (2004) suggested important questions to ask include assessments and determinants of project success or failure. Considering the various arguments within risk management theory, a unified approach is necessary to measure applicability of such theories to current or potential projects. Doing so would help to elucidate the importance of this topic to project managers executing projects and organizations supporting those efforts.

Project Risk Management and Systems of Project Categorization

An indication of the importance of this topic for organizations is the application of risk management theory as measured by project success. Based on the literature, it can be argued that measurement of project objectives such as scope, schedule, budget, and quality can serve as baseline indicators of success (PMI, 2009). Pinto and Slevin (1988) established the concept of categorizing projects, which in turn allowed the direct measurement of success and identification of potential problems. The researchers categorized project success factors as the outcome of budget, schedule, performance, and client satisfaction. Moreover, they realized the importance of measuring projects against such categories to form the basis of a successful project and to identify potential shortcomings or problem areas within the execution or planning of such projects (Pinto & Slevin, 1988).

Freeman and Beale (1992) sought to define and measure project success in terms of both the project manager and the sponsor. This concept integrated the structure of the project into a larger system of business in which projects are categorized not only in terms of the projects themselves but also in terms of the system of sponsorship that led to the inception of those projects. Project categories are recast within the categories of more holistic understandings of business, namely, the understanding of how sponsorship occurs. According to the literature, project sponsors are mostly concerned with performance, budget, and duration, where performance was broken down into scope and quality targets (Freeman & Beale, 1992). Targets of scope were defined as performing all previously defined work and consuming only stated resources. Quality was described by meeting specifications and expectations of project stakeholders. Budget was also a concern and was measured quantitatively in terms of cost.

Raz et al. (2002) linked project success with risk management and the control of uncertainty. The authors' research, although limited, demonstrated "significant phenomena about the use and effectiveness of project risk management techniques" (Raz et al., 2002, p. 107) and project success. In this case, project objectives were measured by specifications, schedule, and budget. The researchers surveyed a series of respondents and concluded risk management practices are indeed positively correlated with meeting budgetary goals in high-uncertainty projects; however, inherently lower risk projects were less likely to be statistically significant (Raz et al., 2002).

Cooke-Davies (2002) sought to identify critical factors that lead to project success, conducting a study that revealed how 30% of these factors (4 out of 12) were related to risk management. Cooke-Davies suggested project success factors include an organization's acceptance of risk management, the assigning ownership of risks, maintaining a risk register, and keeping an up-to-date risk management plan. Additionally, risk management factors were closely correlated to on-time project performance. Cooke-Davies's observations were significant because shared features were established between project risk management and project success. In addition, the research revealed nearly one-third of the factors that lead to project success are factors that directly involve the effective practice of risk management.

Based on both risk management theory and practice (as measured by project success), further review of the literature made evident the ability to categorize risk management processes into six groups. These processes were evaluated in the following categories: (a) planning; (b) identifying; (c) analyzing, both qualitative and quantitative types; (d) responding; and (e) controlling (Krane et al., 2010; PMI, 2009).

Plan Risk Management Process

Cooke-Davies (2002) reported a high correlation between project success and the adequacy of a risk management plan. In other words, project success is greatly influenced by risk management planning. Additionally, Raz and Michael (2001) emphasized that IT projects, in particular, may benefit from project risk management planning. This concept was supported by their survey results. Both Cooke-Davies's and Raz and Michael's studies validated the importance of planning risk management (PMI, 2009). Moreover, Morris and Jamieson (2005) contended project risk management could bridge the gap between strategic management and project management. For example, in the study, 75% of those surveyed found project risk management to be a worthwhile endeavor.

Additionally, Kutsch and Hall (2009) acknowledged PMI's plan risk management process can be complemented by the Office of Government Commerce and the United Kingdom's Association for Project Management standard, finding harmony between multiple risk management standards studied. In contrast, other research revealed numerous project managers do not devote enough time to implementing risk management. One reason given is project managers cannot justify the additional time needed to complete documentation required by the risk management process. Surveys showed nearly one-third of project managers do not include formal project risk management processes in their projects (Kutsch & Hall, 2009).

Success Factors

PMI's standards are not the only significant approaches to risk management. Ward (1999a) presented a generic nine-phase approach to risk management that is complementary to PMI's (2009) risk management standard. In particular, perceived responsibilities and motivation of team members are critical success factors. While more modern frameworks have been developed, lessons learned from human factors, such as ownership, helped to strengthen project risk management planning efforts. According to Mazouz, Facal, and Viola (2008), strategic decision-making became increasingly important for setting risk thresholds and expectations.

Communication

Within the literature, it is recognized a strong risk management plan includes effective communication and documentation. Some researchers suggest an integrated approach to risk management planning must incorporate organizational definitions and strategies (Mikes, 2009). Further examples of risk management planning include the documentation of organizational values, expectations, and consequences of uncertainty. It is stressed both positive and negative aspects of risks should be communicated during the planning process (Csiszar, 2008). Csiszar (2008) further argued that risk-taking is essential for firms to seize the opportunities necessary for optimal profitability and success. According to Hinrichs (2009), transparency in risk management planning has a positive effect in communicating potential risk to the team ahead of time. Hinrichs asserted defining a project's or organization's risk profile up front makes risk tolerance and thresholds better understood, avoiding miscommunication during the execution of the project.

Risk Thresholds

Due to high IT project failure, it can be inferred there is a discrepancy between an organization's acceptable level of risk propensity and project outcome (Islam, 2009). Islam (2009) found more experienced project managers managed risk more effectively. Asnar and Zannone (2008) argued it is necessary to correlate risk attitudes and perceptions in order to create realistic plans of action in relation to organizational rules and policy. Also, Huff and Prybutok (2008) proposed organizations may sometimes document risk thresholds to set expectations. They further defined *risk propensity* as an individual's or organization's appetite to accept or avoid risk.

Stakeholder Management

According to Bourne and Walker (2006), an important aspect of risk management includes stakeholder management, which is often ignored. In the context of risk management, knowledge of individual stakeholders' risk tolerance can ultimately help to set expectations among stakeholders as a whole. Because stakeholders and organizations may view risks differently, Mazouz et al. (2008) found strategic decision-making became increasingly important for setting risk thresholds and expectations. In this case, the plan risk management process can be used as a tool to avoid project failure. Thus, the risk management plan can be seen as a concerted effort to document understanding and expectations. Without adequate stakeholder management, Brook (2005) asserted poor treatment of team members might occur, which can cause poor project performance.

Tailoring Risk Management

Meier (2008) argued larger projects contain inherently more risk than smaller projects and proper planning includes setting expectations. Documented risks include requirement instability, immature technology, and unrealistic project expectations. Additionally, Rosacker and Olson (2008) noted over-simplification of risk management planning should be avoided. Finally, to aid in risk management planning, Reich (2007) emphasized the importance of utilizing knowledge management systems within IT projects to include the capture of risk.

Flyvbjerg (2006) found political and organizational pressures have the ability to obscure real risk management issues. By categorizing and documenting expectations through the risk management plan, such dilemmas may be avoided. Additionally, project planning problems can be traced back to both political and organizational pressure, and can be either real or perceived (Flyvbjerg, 2006). Although categorizing and documenting expectations was found to be effective, Boehm (1991) noted no single approach is sufficient to deal with the complexities of implementing risk management processes in all projects; therefore, an integrated way of thinking about risk and projects is necessary. Key contributions to IT project risk management are therefore necessary to provide a set of processes available at the disposal of the project manager and team. With these processes, teams can make more informed decisions and focus on prioritizing risks for mitigation.

Identify Risks Process

Aubert, Patry, and Rivard (2005) defined *risk* as the outcome, probability, and impact of an undesirable event. One component of impact is budget. Wallace and Keil (2004) found it best to identify and determine risks that affect scope, budget, and schedule up front based on a risk identification framework vetted by several hundred practicing project managers. Therefore, it is important to identify risks and factors that affect a project's bottom line.

Risk Categorization

According to Warkentin et al. (2009), three main categories of risk useful in the process of identifying risk are (a) technical, (b) resource, and (c) organizational, where additional emphasis is placed on organizational risks. It is therefore important to prioritize identifying organizational risks. Further, Chatzoglou and Diamantidis (2009) declared it is important to identify risks in their proper context and provide descriptive information that will allow the calculation of the degree of acceptability that a project ties to each individual risk.

Risk Ownership

Pavlak (2004) believed risk is both necessary and healthy to a project. Thus, teams should strive to take a proactive approach to plan and execute effective risk management versus being reactive. Careful consideration should be placed on high-performing teams that avoid group-think mentality and encourage critical thinking. Engaging the entire team in the risk identification process enables more complete capture of risks.

According to Busby and Zhang (2008), human factors in the risk identification process include the inability to properly identify risk due to inadequate understanding. Inadequate understanding manifests itself through misperception and contradictory beliefs among team members. This conflict results in focusing less on real risks and more on risks that place blame on others. The researchers suggested by including both internal and external threats, bias within the risk identification process could be mitigated.

According to Raz et al. (2002), a key factor for project success was found to be systematic risk identification. While there is an abundance of tools available to perform this task, many project managers choose not to take advantage of these resources. To mitigate these shortcomings, the authors suggested a change of work culture is more effective than a change in risk management tools.

According to Hubbard (2009), a risk matrix is a method for identifying risk. The author found many project managers did not make effective use of a project risk matrix. For example, ineffective risk management includes the inability to tie identified risks to organizational objectives. To mitigate these weaknesses, risk audits may be performed to identify shortcomings and elucidate a future plan of corrective action.

Du, Keil, Mathiassen, Shen, and Tiwana (2007) noted while attention-grabbing risk assessment tools are helpful for novice project managers, these tools should not replace the input of more experienced team members. In this view, Addison (2003) found teams using the Delphi method to identify top IT project risks are more effective. The Delphi method is a technique in which experts independently identify risks that are then tabulated until a consensus is reached. According to Addison, qualified Delphi participants can be utilized to successfully minimize misunderstandings.

Risk Register

In a comprehensive study, Krane et al. (2010) analyzed hundreds of risk elements that make up a so-called *risk register*. Key findings included the correlation between unsuccessful projects and inadequate risk identification. Questions to consider in terms of risk identification included how risks were subcategorized. A major shortcoming was long-term strategic risks were not identified in the majority of projects studied. Finally, the researchers asserted risk identification should not be the sole responsibility of an individual or team but, rather, a shared responsibility including the input of all stakeholders involved.

Cooke-Davies (2002) sought to identify 12 critical success factors within projects. One factor included measuring the level at which risk registers are communicated and updated. Awareness of the risk register is important because even if risks are adequately documented, if they are not disseminated to the team, miscommunication is likely to occur. On the other hand, if the risk register is well communicated but does not contain current information, unnecessary risks could surface.

The risk register includes qualitative risk analysis, which is central to the register's success (Ward, 1999b). Ward (1999b) argued the risk register performs a critical function in the overall documentation and dissemination of individual risk events. These risk events are used as the input to populate project risk probability-impact matrices common within the qualitative risk analysis process. In addition, Williams (1997) stated, over time, project risk management becomes increasingly participative, allowing entire teams the opportunity to contribute to the creation of risk registers and other deliverables. In this case, teams become empowered to improve project success through the use of unbiased risk identification processes. Traditionally, project risk management has not been seen as an overly important process; however, in recent years, project risk management has become increasingly important.

Sanchez, Robert, and Pellerin (2008) stressed the importance of identifying both potential positive and negative risks to a project. For example, positive risk identification includes the capture of risks that would positively benefit the project. Accordingly, while risk identification can focus mainly on negative potential risk events, positive risk events can be equally important to capture in a risk-opportunity register (Sanchez et al., 2008).

Reich (2007) suggested less experienced project managers avoid utilizing project risk management tools such as the risk register. It is therefore suggested the risk register become a focal point in disseminating and collecting risk information from multiple participants. Furthermore, it is asserted that particular focus on internal risk is prudent to establish contingencies for knowledge gaps within the team. Risk register success factors include the continuous updating and assessment of risk throughout the project.

Integration Process

While identifying risks initially can be relatively easy, Raz and Michael (2001) observed tracking and controlling risks throughout the project's life cycle is more challenging. The implication from their study was that no single risk process is sufficient to trump another, and an integrated approach to project risk management must include the integration of all project risk management processes.

According to Royer (2000), many less-experienced project managers do not take the time needed to implement risk identification. It was suggested that comprehensive risk identification techniques include experience-based risk assessments; brainstorming; categorization of risk by severity; and an appropriate mitigation and contingency for high-probability, high-impact risks. Royer also suggested that successful project risk management highly correlates with the likelihood of project success. Utilizing proper risk management identification processes suggests that misunderstandings about risks can be avoided or mitigated. Kajko-Mattsson (2009) emphasized risk identification is not limited to a one-time activity, but may occur throughout a project's life cycle, while Boehm (1991) clarified that no one single approach is sufficient to deal with project risks. It could be argued that teams are better able to make informed decisions and focus on prioritization when risks are identified early on.

Perform Qualitative Risk Analysis Process

According to PMI (2009), perform qualitative risk analysis is "the process of prioritizing risks for further analysis or action by assessing and combining their probability of occurrence and impact" (p. 110). Raz et al. (2002) stated, "There is no such thing as a risk free project" (p. 101), and that factors for project success include probabilistic analysis." Raz and Michael (2001) identified several qualitative risk analysis tools, including (a) probability assessment, (b) impact assessment, (c) time-frame assessment, (d) classification, and (e) ranking. Shenhar (2001) recommended that project managers weigh risks consistently for a balanced risk management approach.

Perminova et al. (2007) argued qualitative risk management methods involving personal skill and judgment are highly effective in identifying risk. A cause-and-effect relationship can document potential positive and negative events ahead of time. It is clear qualitative risk management is an evolving practice that has become increasingly standardized, to the benefit of its practitioners.

Probability and Impact

According to Mulcahy (2010), qualitative risk analysis includes subjective evaluation of probability and impact of risk. By performing this analysis, a short list of critical risks can be identified for management or mitigation planning. Since even ranked probability and impact are subjective, it is important to document team and stakeholder agreements on the definition of risk.

Mulcahy (2010) noted the goal of a probability-impact matrix is to first calculate the individual risk scores, then rank each project's risks against each other. The risk score is generally made up of a risk probability and impact measured on a scale of one to 10. In this system, probability is generally rated low between one and two, medium between three and four, medium-high between five and six, high between seven and eight, and 100% certain between nine and 10.

Hillson (2009) noted the importance of identifying high-, medium-, and low-priority categories using a probability-impact matrix. These zones are often color coded to allow easy categorization. Scores are negative if the risk is a threat and positive if the risk is an opportunity. The results of this assessment are documented in a risk register, along with evidence justifying a risk's score and relative ranking. Ward (1999b) explained one of the most common qualitative risk assessment scoring methods is the probability-impact matrix. Risk rankings are calculated by multiplying each risk's probability by its impact, making risk classification less subjective. In general, risks ranked highest are prime candidates for mitigation. Rankings can be translated into categories of high, medium, or low risk. Ward argued this method is both schedule and budget effective, though limited in scope. Outputs of this method include updates to the risk register.

Mulcahy (2010) stated that similar to probability measurements, impact measurements typically consist of a rating from one to 10. Impact scales are more complex but can range from a rating of one, with no real impact to the project objective, to 10, indicating project failure. Impact ratings between two and nine may indicate an exceeded budget or delayed project. Mulcahy indicated the importance of considering a risk's individual impact on the project. A risk's score is calculated by multiplying its probability by its impact. Using this method, the score for a particular risk could be described as between one and 100.

According to Mulcahy (2010), one may determine the riskiness of a particular project by summing the individual risk scores and dividing that sum by the number of risks. The overall risk score may be compared with the organization's risk appetite to determine if a project is too risky to move forward. However, Mulcahy noted the primary value of calculating risk scores is to determine a project's top risks. It is prudent to plan appropriate risk response and mitigation to address a project's highest scoring risks. Since it may not be possible to plan for every risk, the prudent approach is to tackle these high-probability, high-impact risks first.

Pyra and Trask (2002) posited a risk priority matrix is a beneficial qualitative analysis tool to compare risk probability to impact. The authors further suggested categorization of risks should include both internal and external factors. Their case study showed while external risks stayed relatively constant over time, internal risks tended to decrease over time, especially when mitigation strategies were implemented (Pyra & Trask, 2002).

Shortcomings of Qualitative Risk Analysis

Williams (1996) called into question probability-impact analysis performed in qualitative risk analysis. According to the author, one should proceed with caution when calculating risk on only two dimensions. Cox (2008) pointed out that qualitative risk analysis, used in risk matrices, can present an incomplete picture since risk cannot be measured and compared quantitatively. Additionally, according to Boehm (1991), it is important to note while probability-impact calculations are beneficial, a certain amount of uncertainty will always be present according to its qualitative nature.

Perform Quantitative Risk Analysis Process

According to PMI (2009), *perform quantitative risk analysis* is "the process of numerically analyzing the effect of identified risks on project objectives" (p. 110). Mulcahy (2010) stated that quantitative risk analysis is a calculation of overall project risk, often including budget impact, whereas qualitative risk analysis focuses on individual risks. Due to the more complex nature of quantitative risk analysis, it may not be suitable for every project. It is a critical prerequisite to identify all project risks before performing quantitative risk analysis. If all risks are not identified, there is a danger of incomplete conclusions.

Mulcahy (2010) suggested the most common method of calculating quantitative risk is probability multiplied by monetary impact. Positive or negative quantitative risk sums threats and opportunities, providing a measured overall project budget. Similar to qualitative analysis, quantitative risk may be either positive or negative. Additionally, Mulcahy suggested models can be developed that express risks and their expected impact on the project schedule. For example, if given both the expected cost of risk and its associated impact, one can determine whether the risk fits a project's budget and schedule constraints. If it is acceptable to move forward despite the risk, no further risk management actions need be taken. However, if a risk's impact is unacceptable, that risk may be added to a risk response plan.

Combinatorial Effects

According to Hillson (2009), while qualitative risk analysis considers individual risks, quantitative risk analysis focuses on the combined effect of all project risks, particularly in terms of budget and schedule. Since threats and opportunities are often overlooked in this process, it is important to include both in a complete assessment. Potential issues surrounding quantitative risk analysis include data quality and interpretation. Additionally, according to Baccarini and Archer (2001), quantitative risk management includes project risk ranking and the risks' overall effects. In this paradigm, the project's riskiness is assessed and can be used for both historical assessment and future project selection.

Numerical Models

According to Dunkel and Weber (2007), a key benefit of Monte Carlo analysis is robust statistical risk analysis. Such simulations are highly flexible in modeling multiple measurements and suited especially for high-value projects requiring extraordinary amounts of due diligence. Miranda and Abran (2008) stated that sophisticated quantitative risk management utilizing Monte Carlo analysis results in the ability to discern risk level among a portfolio of projects. Projects least likely to experience cost overruns may be preferred over those that are more likely. A chief benefit of this technique is that it is run in simulation, and management may be able to make adjustments to plans prior to project acceptance. Miranda and Abran postulated that while small projects may experience under-budgeting, larger projects suffer from over-budgeting and over-engineering.

Regev, Shtub, and Ben-Haim (2006) assessed the weaknesses and limitations of the Monte Carlo technique. These limitations included high setup costs and inaccurate forecasting by inexperienced practitioners. Alternatives to quantitative risk analysis, such as non-statistical methods, were cited. Regardless of the approach, the researchers determined that it is better to be proactive than reactive. Pollack-Johnson and Liberatore (2005) performed a study that revealed approximately 20% of commercially available project management software includes Monte Carlo simulation capabilities. As an alternative to the Monte Carlo technique, critical path analysis assesses the impact of unknown events.

In a survey, Voetsch et al. (2004) found quantitative risk analysis tools such as Monte Carlo analysis and other complex techniques were neither widely used nor strongly supported among organizations. The authors noted that attempting to make quantitative risk analysis fit all projects and all organizations might not be effective.

McLain (2009) described a quantitative method in which relationships between tasks could be assessed. However, it was found that uncertainty could not always be calculated precisely because it is not always possible to account for all variations and dependencies. Finally, Jackson and Al-Hamdani (2008) suggested that quantitative risk analysis entails a summation of risks, compared with an acceptable risk threshold, determining whether a project should move forward.

Plan Risk Response Process

According to PMI (2009), the plan risk response process is "the process of developing options and actions to enhance opportunities and to reduce threats to project objectives" (p. 110). The purpose of this process is to document and determine the set of actions that will most likely increase the chance of project success within its given constraints. Naturally, this process takes place once all risks have been identified, analyzed, and prioritized. Finally, it is understood not all risks will need a response.

Additionally, according to PMI (2009), it is not practical or feasible to eliminate all threats from a project. Therefore, the level and detail of planned risk responses should be determined by an organization's risk appetite. The organization's risk appetite must be clearly identified and communicated before starting this activity. PMI stated that risk response strategies include one or more of the following: (a) avoid a threat or exploit an opportunity, (b) transfer a threat or share an opportunity, (c) mitigate a threat or enhance an opportunity, or (d) accept a threat or opportunity.

Strategies

According to Mulcahy (2010), expert opinions can include the following: using less complex processes, adding time, increasing redundancy, outsourcing, postponing activities, or scheduling activities earlier. It was noted each approach is specific to the risk being mitigated and subject to the opinion of an expert.

Hillson (2009) stated risk response planning is one of the most important risk management processes because it allows the team to face risk strategically, plan responses, and assign ownership. When planning risk responses, it is important to consider resource, cost, and response effectiveness. It is also important to be aware that responding to a risk may introduce a secondary risk.

Rush and Vednere (2008) asserted that for critical and highly probable risks, a mitigation strategy should be determined. Within this strategy, a given risk response should have clearly defined controls and procedures. Mitigation is specific to a given risk, and it is suggested that lessons learned from risk modeling can be beneficial in creating an initial response.

According to Addison and Vallabh (2002), risk management is exemplified in taking strategic and specific counter-measures to prevent or mitigate identified risks. By mitigating identified risks, a project's risk exposure can be reduced and quality increased. It is the opinion of the authors the high failure rate of IT projects is caused by failure to take cautious measures to mitigate risk. The authors postulated that frequent and periodic risk assessment is a precursor to planning risk responses that improve a project's success.

Risk Register Updates

Mulcahy (2010) stated the output of planned risk responses includes updating the risk register, which documents final triggers, response plans, and contingencies for each risk. Solicitation of expert opinion is recommended to determine the most appropriate action for each risk and assignment of risk owners.

Action Owners

Hinrichs (2009) stated after risks have been assessed, it is necessary to establish accountability for those risks ranked critical. This accountability could include mitigating, discontinuing, or sharing the risk with another party. In this way, accountability for identified risks can be achieved, resulting in a plan of action to address, understand, and manage high-priority risks. Ownership of project risks should be traceable to senior management through escalation and organizational policy.

According to Raz et al. (2002), the risk response planning process is a precursor to contingency analysis, which reveals options for mitigation of risk ahead of project execution. On the other hand, the researchers found organizations tended to be over-optimistic and did not execute risk management processes with complete effectiveness. They observed project risk management has not yet fully become part of the culture of project management.

Project Management Plan Updates

An important aspect of IT project risk management practices include the concept that risk response planning is proportional to the impact and likelihood of a given risk (Barki, Rivard, & Talbot, 2001). Adopting a contingency perspective implies having a high level of understanding of project tasks and dependencies in order to plan appropriately. The authors suggested, as a best practice, the level and frequency of communication depends on a project's individual risks and overall level of uncertainty.

According to Ben-David and Raz (2001), risk response planning is one of the most significant project risk management processes. The net effect of this planning is for predictive risk reduction. For example, specific premeditated actions can be developed and implemented according to individual risks identified. It was noted an occasional tradeoff will be made when planning for risk reduction, especially when considering necessary budget, schedule, or resources (Ben-David & Raz, 2001).

Success Factors

Keil, Cule, Lyytinen, and Schmidt (1998) stated that "software projects are notoriously difficult to manage and too many of them end in failure" (p. 79). In a Delphi experiment, they noted that within three independent panels, a common set of 11 risk factors were identified as the most important items to address. The study was designed to identify which factors IT project managers perceived as risks and to identify if these risks could be categorized for proper mitigation. Three factors found to mitigate project risk the most included resolving lack of management commitment, securing user commitment, and clarifying unclear requirements.

Boehm (1991) identified key principles for project risk management success, which included tools and techniques at the disposal of the project manager. With a unified set of tools and techniques, teams can make better informed decisions and focus on prioritized risks for mitigation and planning purposes. A top 10 risk and mitigation matrix was created based on the needs of the team; however, such lists may be unique to each project and industry.

Monitor and Control Risk Process

PMI (2009) stated for each previously identified project risk for which a contingency plan has been identified, a corresponding set of triggered conditions should be specified. It is the responsibility of the individual or project manager to effectively monitor and carry out mitigation measures as they occur within a project. The prerequisite steps of planned risk management identify risk and perform qualitative and quantitative risk management alongside planned risk responses. Moreover, within monitoring and controlling risks, stakeholder communication is very important (PMI, 2009).

Tracking

Monitoring and controlling risks need not generate excessive project overhead, according to PMI (2009), as long as the prior processes have been adequately planned. According to PMI, tracking of project risks fits squarely within standard project monitoring and controlling processes, further minimizing overhead. Additionally, within this process, monitoring risk trigger conditions, maintaining risk awareness, and managing contingency reserves were found to be important. The tracking of compliance and documentation of results of monitor and control risk processes were fundamental outputs. Consolidated information should be archived for historical purposes and benefit future projects.

Boehm (1991) asserted that proper monitoring and controlling processes include the tracking of a project's top 10 risk items on a weekly, monthly, or milestone basis. The author suggested that appropriate follow-up, reassessment, or corrective action is an outcome of such monitoring and tracking efforts. Risk monitoring and controlling, therefore, complements the prior work performed in risk identification ranking and analysis and provides a framework to prevent identified risks from spiraling out of control.

Reporting

Hillson (2009), contrary to other authors, did not define a monitor and control risk process. However, well-defined risk identification and assessment were found to be critical for risk response planning. Monitor and control risks could therefore best be described as risk communication and risk review as utilized throughout a project. Finally, Hillson recommended capturing lessons learned, including those within the monitoring and controlling process, as an important exercise in documentation and communication for future projects.

Organizational Processes

A central theme Mulcahy (2010) discussed is that effective monitor and control risk processes are dependent on time and dedication spent on prior risk management processes. Therefore, prerequisites to successful project risk management monitoring and control include adequate time spent on upstream risk identification, qualitative or quantitative risk analysis, and plan risk response process. Mulcahy further pointed out many project managers do not effectively understand or perform control. One key recommendation is the performing of risk reviews in order to control risks and manage change. These reviews may take place on a regular basis and may be prospective in nature. In some cases, a risk review board may be used to assess objectively and comment on a project's risk performance. Risk audits, on the other hand, look back in time to what has occurred, while risk reviews focus on future events. Throughout the monitor and control risk process, any changes to project risk should be documented in the updates and refinement of the risk register. Communicating risk to stakeholders is an integral part of monitoring and controlling risks. Example communication methods may include reports, status updates, a risk register, or other forms of communication (Mulcahy, 2010).

Voetsch et al. (2004) observed that organizational support for risk monitoring and control varies by organization to the extent some managers support reporting of risk more than others. The implication is without adequate transparency, risk monitoring and control will become less effective if project managers are afraid to communicate identified risks within this process.

Communication

According to Mulcahy (2010), communicating top risks on a frequent basis helps to keep team members focused and enhances the effectiveness of dealing with issues before they occur. Finally, lessons learned should be compiled at the end of a project in order to help prevent similar issues from occurring in future projects to continuously improve process and ultimately save time and money on future projects.

Observations

Raz and Michael (2001) made an important observation that while it may be relatively easy to identify risks in the beginning of a project through the use of specified tools and techniques, it is a more complicated endeavor to monitor and control risks in the absence of governance or standardization. Examples of project risk monitoring and control include analysis of deviations and exceptions, closing risks, risk status, and trend reporting.

According to the research, gaps have been found in executive support of risk management (Ingley & Walt, 2008). The significance of these findings is cautionary in that strong stakeholder support is essential for proper risk monitoring and control; otherwise, reporting could have a null effect (Ingley & Walt, 2008).

Freimut et al. (2001) found approximately 20% of controlling actions were related to the reduction of risk. Forty-four participants were unable to assess the impact of their performance of controlling risks.

In two case studies analyzed, Kontio, Getto, and Landes (1998) found management focus has shifted from pure risk identification as a main organizational focus to now include risk monitoring and controlling. As monitoring and controlling methods mature within the organization, it is expected that compliance will become increasingly robust and important.

Chapter Summary

Ever-increasing project complexity requires new ways to manage projects effectively given uncertainty, ushering in a new paradigm within project management theory (Laufer et al., 1996). This shift within the practice of simultaneous management necessitates a focused approach to risk management, according to the scholars. Second, by categorizing the measurement of project success, factors affecting overall performance, either positively or negatively, allow a granular approach to assessing successful outcomes (Pinto & Slevin, 1988). Combining focus on project risk management practices and their related impacts on project success, researchers proposed a methodological approach including planning, identifying, performing analysis, and responding to project risk (Aubert et al., 2005; Cooke-Davies, 2002; Mulcahy, 2010; Pinto & Slevin, 1988; PMI, 2009).

CHAPTER 3. METHODOLOGY

Introduction

The purpose of the research was to examine the relationship between the utilization of project risk management processes and IT project success. In addition, mediating variables were examined to understand supplemental project success drivers, which may complement the understanding of the study's dependent and independent variables. Overall, the data gathered will help to elucidate a better understanding of the significance of project risk management theory in IT projects for the benefit of project management practitioners, stakeholders, and the body of knowledge.

Research Design

The study used a non-experimental, descriptive research design to explore the relationship between utilization of project risk management processes and IT project success. A quantitative survey instrument (see Appendix) was provided to a subset of project managers who are self-identified as IT project managers within the SurveyMonkey database. Since it would have been prohibitive to perform a population census in this case, probability sampling was utilized for statistical generalization of the larger group. This research design was suitable since the independent variables were not controlled and no treatment provided or requested by the participants.

Sample

The population for this study consisted of targeted individuals who are self-identified as project managers from within the SurveyMonkey database. SurveyMonkey was chosen because of its unique ability to quickly and efficiently target audience members and align to the study's constraints. Because survey participants were prescreened, the SurveyMonkey population was well suited for the goals of the study.

The sample size needed was calculated for an infinite population using the formula $N = [(Z)^2 (p)(1 - p)] \div c^2$, where N is the sample size needed, given (Z) the confidence level, (p) percentage picking a choice, and (c) the confidence interval. For this survey, the confidence level (Z) was set at 1.96 for 95%, the percentage picking a choice (p) set to .5 for 50%, and the confidence interval (c) set to .05 (± 5%) to give a sample size required of $N = [(1.96)^2(.5)(1 - .5)] \div .05^2 =$ 384 survey participants. Based on a hypothetical 5% survey response rate, the instrument had to reach at least 7,680 potential participants in order to achieve 384 completed responses.

Setting

The setting for this study was the secure online environment, which was presented to prequalified participants within the SurveyMonkey database. SurveyMonkey was contracted to present the survey instrument and enable the gathering of completed results up to 384 participants, as requested for the study's sample size calculation. SurveyMonkey performed sampling by electronically distributing the Institutional Review Board (IRB)-approved survey instrument to qualified participants in its database. The survey was voluntary, could be exited at any time, and was designed to exclusively avoid the capture of personally identifiable information.

Instrumentation

A survey instrument (see Appendix) was developed for this study based on background questions on the topic of project risk management processes and IT project success. Since a new instrument was created, a field test was performed, followed by IRB approval of a pilot study. The results of the field test and pilot study were incorporated into the final survey instrument. Dependent and independent variables were coded into the instrument design to allow for data analysis.

Data Collection

Following approval from Capella University's IRB, the survey instrument was privately posted to SurveyMonkey and traffic initiated from within the SurveyMonkey website to enable data collection. Permission and Informed Consent were included as a preface to the survey, at which point the participant could opt out. Participants were expected to complete the survey electronically in one session. Participants were chosen and preselected exclusively from within the SurveyMonkey database. Neither personally identifiable data, such as participant or project name, nor the companies they work for were recorded.

A web-based survey was used for this study to tabulate and track responses from participants and included a mix of questions with nominal dichotomous (yes/no) answers as well as continuous and interval type questions. The survey instrument was validated through a pre-survey field test, with knowledgeable experts for further refinement, prior to the release of the actual instrument to the target population IT project practitioners in the SurveyMonkey database.

Data Analysis

SPSS descriptive statistics were used to visually display the results of the survey instrument and included histograms, scatter plots, and summary statistics such as mean. Hypothesis testing and establishing the correlation between variables were examined through the use of statistical analysis, including logistic regression, frequency, and percentage calculations.

In order to form a basis for project success, metrics were collected and defined in the context inside or outside of a 15% variance in a planned versus actual budget, schedule, or scope metric. For example, had a project come within 15% (0–15% variance) of a project's planned versus actual budget, a score of success for that metric would have been recorded. In the same regard, had a project's planned versus actual budget exceeded 15% (over 15% variance), a score of nonsuccess for that metric would have been recorded. Since three success scores were calculated for each survey, a combination of success and nonsuccess factors were recorded as a delimiting factor. For example, a project could be scored successful as within budget but not within schedule or scope. Other combinations were possible, depending on how the survey participant answered the questions.

For Research Question 1, three regressions were conducted to examine the extent to which project risk management processes (planning, identifying, qualitative, quantitative, responding, and controlling) predict each of the three outcome variables (budget, schedule, and scope). The resulting statistics included an odds ratio for each predictor for each outcome variable and an R^2 for each regression.

For Research Question 2, three regressions were conducted to examine the extent to which project management demographics (project success and project manager experience, certification, level of education, project size, type, and duration) predict each of the three dichotomous outcome variables (budget, schedule, and scope). The resulting statistics included an odds ratio for each predictor for each outcome variable and an R^2 for each regression.

For Research Question 3, three chi-square difference tests were used. The first chi-square difference test, using budget as the outcome variable, was between Research Question 1 chi-square and Research Question 2 chi-square. The second chi-square difference test, using schedule as the outcome variable, was between Research Question 1 chi-square and Research Question 2 chi-square. The third chi-square difference test, using scope as the outcome variable, was between Research Question 1 chi-square and Research Question 2 chi-square.

Statistical analyses used for the research questions are shown in Table 2.

Table 2. Variables and Statistics for Research Questions.

Research question	Variables	Statistical analysis
R_1. To what extent is utilization of project risk management processes (planning, identifying, qualitative, quantitative, responding, and controlling) related to project success outcomes (budget, schedule, and scope)?	Dependent Budget Schedule Scope Independent Planning Identifying Qualitative Quantitative Responding Controlling	Regressions
R_2. What is the correlation between reported project success and project manager experience, certification, level of education and project size, type and duration?	Dependent Budget Schedule Scope Demographic Project size Project type Project duration Project manager experience Project manager certification Project manager education	Regressions
R_3. Does the utilization of project risk management processes correlate with project success more than project manager experience, certification, level of education, and project size, type, or duration?	Budget Schedule Scope	χ^2

Validity and Reliability

Validity

Fowler (2002) reported the four main reasons survey respondents respond with less-than-valid answers are (a) they did not understand the question, (b) they did not know the answer, (c) they did not remember the answer, or (d) they did not want to report the response. In responding to these threats, sensitivity to survey takers' understanding, recollection, or personal bias were considered in the context of validity. To combat a misunderstanding of the question, definitions for unusual words or phrases were included in the survey as needed. In the event a survey taker did not want to report his or her responses, the survey made it clear the individual could exit the survey at any time and choose not to have any responses recorded.

According to Cooper and Schindler (2006), validity of a sample depends on both accuracy and precision. *Accuracy* is described as a primary reduction of bias from the sample, whereas *precision* is measured by how closely the sample represents the population. In this study, threats to accuracy were combated through the use of clear language that avoids bias or judgment. Threats to precision included thoughtful selection of the target population, in addition to ensuring an adequate number of respondents answered all survey questions.

A field test was used to assess face validity, determine readability, the total amount of time to take the survey, and other feedback. Subject matter experts were asked to review and provide feedback on the instrument. These test takers were recognized experts in the field of project risk management and not simply general practitioners of project management.

Reliability

Reliability, sometimes referred to as *repeatability*, aims to create an environment in which there is a "consistent data collection experience" (Fowler, 2002, p. 78). Subsequent to the field test, a pilot study was submitted for IRB approval. The aim of both the field test and pilot study was to ensure repeatability, consistency, and psychometric soundness. The field test utilized noted project risk management experts, while the pilot study was conducted among a selected set of IT project managers from within a select SurveyMonkey population. For the pilot study, Cronbach's alpha was used to analyze survey constructs for confidence levels and reliability.

When the pilot study was completed, out of 22 survey responses, 19 were validated as complete and three were omitted as incomplete, for a survey completion rate of 86.36%. The average time to complete a survey was 13.79 minutes. At the end of the survey, the following optional question was asked, "Were any of the questions ambiguous or unclear, and if so, can you explain briefly?" Twelve of the 22 participants provided feedback to this question, 100% of whom indicated there were no ambiguous or unclear questions in the survey.

SPSS 20 was used to calculate Cronbach's alpha as .970 (N = 19 with 40 variables) for the study variables. Possible limitations are the small sample, as this reflected a pilot study and the use of nonparametric dichotomous/nominal variables.

Due to the results of the pilot study participant feedback, survey completion rate, and high Cronbach's alpha, no changes were made to the instrument.

Ethical Considerations

Ethical considerations for this study addressed participant privacy and confidentiality, benefits and risks, vulnerable populations considerations, and data security. Each of these areas was addressed as follows. In terms of participant privacy and confidentiality, participants were assured the survey instrument would collect no personally identifiable information from participants. Other than demographic information, neither participant names, company names, nor project names were collected. Individuals were not tracked or tagged, and only aggregate statistical data were published, ensuring both confidentiality and privacy.

Regarding benefits and risks, the possibility that aggregate survey data could be traced to an individual survey participant or company was minimal. Individual survey results were not published and were maintained on a password-protected computer system. The resultant findings of the study should not cause any undue psychological or emotional harm. It is understood that findings of the study will benefit the body of knowledge in the practice of project risk management, such that even if negative findings are reported, they would outweigh any potential harm from such findings.

In terms of vulnerable populations and considerations, it was determined that there are no such population groups in the study. All participants were of adult age and screened by years of job experience. Since no personally identifiable information was collected, there was no harm to individuals or employers through the use of individual survey responses.

Data security included the private collection of individual survey responses for aggregate statistical analysis. Access to survey responses was governed by a single secure password-protected website at the start of the study, with information downloaded to a secured computer system for analysis. After a period of five years, any data stored on the secure website, accessible to only the researcher, will be removed.

CHAPTER 4. RESULTS

Introduction

The purpose of this study was to understand whether utilizing project risk management processes correlates with improved IT project success as measured by self-reported variance in planned versus actual end-of-project budget, schedule, and scope.

While a large volume of literature has been written on generalized factors involved in project success, few studies have examined the relationship between the use of project risk management processes and actual project success as measured by project outcomes—thus, this study was conducted.

The following primary research question was addressed in this study:

R_1. To what extent is utilization of project risk management processes (planning, identifying, qualitative, quantitative, responding, and controlling) related to project success outcomes (budget, schedule, and scope)?

In addition, the following subsidiary research questions were asked in support of the primary research question:

R_2. What is the correlation between reported project success and project manager experience, certification, level of education, and project size, type, and duration?

R_3. Does the utilization of project risk management processes correlate with project success more than project manager experience, certification, level of education, and project size, type, or duration?

A literature review was conducted to ascertain risk management elements that might affect project success the most. Based on this review, a survey instrument was developed and pilot tested prior to being used as part of the main study. The remainder of this chapter includes a description of the population and sample followed by details of analysis and results organized by research question.

Population and Sample

The study examined responses from 78 participants. Frequencies and percentages were conducted on the demographic survey items. Participant demographics are presented in Table 3.

Table 3. Participant Demographics

Variable	n	%
IT project job function or title		
Project manager	31	40
Project coordinator	6	8
Project analyst	13	17
Project leader	13	17
Other	15	19
Job status on previous assignment		
Contractor	14	18
Employee	60	77
Other	4	5
Time spent managing IT projects		
Up to half-time	25	32
More than half-time but less than full-time	19	24
Full-time	34	44
Work location		
North America, United States	72	92
Europe, Middle East, Africa	2	3
Latin America	2	3
Other	2	3
Customer location		
North America, United States	69	89
Europe, Middle East, Africa	3	4
Asia, Pacific	2	3
Latin America	2	3
Other	2	3
Company focus		
Airlines, aerospace, defense	2	3
Automotive	2	3
Construction	4	5
Education	4	5

Variable	n	%
Entertainment	2	3
Financial services	8	10
Government	5	6
Health care, pharmaceuticals	8	10
Information technology	31	40
Insurance	1	1
Nonprofit	3	4
Retail, consumer, electronics	6	8
Utilities, energy	2	3
Highest level college degree		
No degree	6	8
Associate's degree	6	8
Bachelor's degree	40	51
Master's degree	25	32
Doctoral degree	1	1
How long ago did the selected IT project finish		
Within last 2 years	63	81
More than 2 years ago	15	19
Number of people that dedicated half their time to project		
Up to 4	28	36
5–10	15	32
11–20	10	13
20+	15	19
Total duration of IT project		
Up to 3 months	9	12
More than 3 but less than 6 months	21	27
More than 6 but less than 12 months	30	38
More than 12 months	18	23
Total cost of IT project (in USD)		
Up to $100,000	26	33
More than $100,000 but less than $500,000	21	27

Variable	n	%
More than $500,000 but less than $1,000,000	17	22
More than $1,000,000	14	18
Employer		
Up to 100 people	15	19
101–500 people	20	26
501–1,000 people	8	10
1,001–5,000 people	11	14
5,001–10,000 people	7	9
More than 10,000 people	17	22
Customer base		
Up to 100 people	10	13
101–500 people	10	13
501–1,000 people	10	13
1,001–5,000 people	16	21
5,001–10,000 people	10	13
More than 10,000 people	22	28
IT project worked on		
Software	67	86
Hardware	26	33
Services	28	36
Other	5	6
Qualification(s) or certification(s) earned		
American Academy of Project Management (AAPM)	3	4
Capability Maturity Model Integration (CMMI)	7	9
Certificate in Project Management	15	19
Certificate in Risk Management	6	8
Certified Associate in Project Management (CAPM)	6	8
Information Technology Infrastructure Library (ITIL)	19	24
Lean Six Sigma	6	8
PMI Agile Certified Practitioner	4	5

Variable	n	%
(PMI-ACP) PMI Risk Management Professional (PMI-RMP)	2	3
PMI Scheduling Professional (PMI-SP)	2	3
Program Management Professional (PgMP)	5	6
Project Management Professional (PMP)	16	21
CompTIA Project+	6	8
Projects in Controlled Environments (PRINCE2)	3	4
Six Sigma Black Belt	3	4
Six Sigma Green Belt	3	4
None of the above	35	45
Years of experience		
IT project management		
Up to 2 years	9	12
More than 2 and up to 4 years	14	18
More than 4 and up to 6 years	13	17
More than 6 and up to 8 years	11	14
More than 8 years	23	30
None	8	10
IT project risk management		
Up to 2 years	16	21
More than 2 and up to 4 years	15	19
More than 4 and up to 6 years	8	10
More than 6 and up to 8 years	6	8
More than 8 years	14	18
None	19	24
Resource management		
Up to 2 years	8	10
More than 2 and up to 4 years	7	9
More than 4 and up to 6 years	13	17
More than 6 and up to 8 years	11	14
More than 8 years	18	23

Variable	n	%
None	21	27
Technical management		
Up to 2 years	5	6
More than 2 and up to 4 years	7	9
More than 4 and up to 6 years	12	15
More than 6 and up to 8 years	11	14
More than 8 years	26	33
None	17	22

Note. Percentages may not total 100% due to rounding error and participant allowance to select multiple responses.

Many participants held a project manager position (31, 40%) and worked full-time managing their projects (34, 44%). The majority of participants were employees on their previous assignments (66, 70%) and worked in North America/United States (72, 92%). Many participants reported their company's focus was IT (31, 40%). Most participants held a bachelor's degree (40, 51%) and finished their project within the last two years (63, 81%). Twenty-five (32%) participants indicated they had 5–10 people who dedicated at least half their time to the project, and 21 (27%) participants indicated the project took more than three months but less than six months and cost more than $100,000 but less than $500,000. Most participants worked in software for the IT project (67, 86%). Many participants indicated they had not earned any of the listed qualifications or certifications

(35, 45%) or had spent more than 8 years in technical management (26, 33%).

Details of Analysis and Results

Descriptive Statistics

Eleven variables were examined in the study: planning, identifying, qualitative, quantitative, responding, controlling, certification, experience, budget, schedule, and scope. In order to form a basis for project success, metrics were collected and defined in the context inside or outside of a 15% variance in a planned versus actual budget, schedule, or scope metric. Budget, schedule, and scope were each treated as dichotomous variables (0 = more than 15% under/more than 15% over vs. 1 = within 15% of original/no variance). The remaining eight variables were treated as composite scores. Cronbach's alpha tests of reliability were conducted on the eight composite scores. Descriptive statistics on the eight composite scores are presented in Table 4.

Table 4. Descriptive Statistics for the Eight Composite Scores

Variable	α	No. items	M	SD
Planning	.92	8	0.50	0.40
Identifying	.85	8	0.54	0.34
Qualitative	.82	4	0.54	0.40
Quantitative	.86	7	0.38	0.35
Responding	.87	6	0.50	0.38
Controlling	.85	7	0.43	0.36
Certification	.62	17	1.81	1.85
Experience	.82	4	3.89	1.35

Reliabilities, expressed as alpha coefficients, ranged from .62 (certification) to .92 (planning), indicating questionable to excellent reliability (George & Mallery, 2010). Means and standard deviations were also conducted on the eight variables, where experience scores had the largest mean ($M = 3.89$), followed by certification scores ($M = 1.81$).

Research Question 1

Research Question 1 asked, to what extent is utilization of project risk management processes (planning, identifying, qualitative, quantitative, responding, and controlling) related to project success outcomes (budget, schedule, and scope)?

To address Research Question 1, three binary logistic regression analyses were conducted to determine if the independent variables (planning, identifying, qualitative, quantitative, responding, and controlling) predict the dependent variable (budget, schedule, and scope); one regression was conducted per dependent variable. Statistical significance was determined at α = .05. The results of the logistic regression analyses are presented in Table 5.

The first logistic regression was conducted on the budget variable, and the results were not statistically significant, $\chi^2(6)$ = 4.74, p = .578, Nagelkerke R^2 = .09, suggesting the use of project risk management tools and techniques within planning, identifying, qualitative, quantitative, responding, and controlling processes could not predict if the IT project would be completed within budget. No statistical significance exists.

Table 5. Logistic Regression Models on Budget, Schedule, and Scope as Compared to Planning, Identifying, Qualitative, Quantitative, Responding, and Controlling

Source	B	SE	Wald	df	p	OR
Budget						
Planning	-0.78	1.40	0.31	1	.576	0.46
Identifying	-0.22	1.35	0.03	1	.870	0.80
Qualitative	0.46	1.59	0.08	1	.774	1.58
Quantitative	2.07	1.41	2.14	1	.143	7.91
Responding	1.55	1.76	0.78	1	.378	4.73
Controlling	-3.23	1.84	3.07	1	.080	0.04
Schedule						
Planning	-0.29	1.32	0.05	1	.827	0.75
Identifying	0.20	1.30	0.03	1	.875	1.23
Qualitative	0.83	1.40	0.35	1	.556	2.28

Source	B	SE	Wald	df	p	OR
Quantitative	0.06	1.37	0.00	1	.963	1.07
Responding	0.57	1.49	0.15	1	.704	1.76
Controlling	-1.29	1.54	0.70	1	.402	0.27
Scope						
Planning	1.40	1.65	0.72	1	.397	4.05
Identifying	0.91	1.64	0.31	1	.578	2.49
Qualitative	0.49	1.49	0.11	1	.744	1.63
Quantitative	-3.11	1.82	2.92	1	.087	0.04
Responding	-0.87	1.64	0.28	1	.596	0.42
Controlling	0.31	1.59	0.04	1	.845	1.36

Note. Budget: $\chi^2(6)$ = 4.74, p = .578, Nagelkerke R^2 = .09. Schedule: $\chi^2(6)$ = 1.07, p = .983, Nagelkerke R^2 = .02. Scope: $\chi^2(6)$ = 5.54, p = .476, Nagelkerke R^2 = .10.

The second logistic regression was conducted on the schedule variable, and the results were not statistically significant, $\chi^2(6) = 1.07$, $p = .983$, Nagelkerke $R^2 = .02$, suggesting the use of project risk management tools and techniques within planning, identifying, qualitative, quantitative, responding, and controlling processes could not predict if the IT project would be completed within schedule. No statistical significance exists.

The third logistic regression was conducted on the scope variable, and the results were not statistically significant, $\chi^2(6) = 5.54$, $p = .476$, Nagelkerke $R^2 = .10$, suggesting the use of project risk management tools and techniques within planning, identifying, qualitative, quantitative, responding, and controlling processes could not predict if the IT project would be completed within scope. No statistical significance exists. The null hypothesis – there is no statistical relationship between the utilization of project risk management processes (planning, identifying, qualitative, quantitative, responding, controlling) and project success outcomes (budget, schedule, scope) – cannot be rejected.

Research Question 2

Research Question 2 asked, what is the correlation between reported project success and project manager experience, certification, level of education, and project size, type, and duration?

To address Research Question 2, three binary logistic regression analyses were conducted to determine if the independent variables (experience, certification, education, project size, type, and duration) effectively predict the dependent variable (budget, schedule, and scope); one regression was conducted per dependent variable. Education, project size, and duration were dichotomized based on a median split. Statistical significance was determined at $\alpha = .05$. The results of the logistic regression analyses are presented in Table 6.

Table 6. Logistic Regression Models on Budget, Schedule, and
Scope as Compared to Experience, Certification, Education, Project
Size, Type, and Duration

Source	B	SE	Wald	df	p	OR
Budget						
Experience	0.13	0.22	0.33	1	.566	1.14
Certi-fication	-0.29	0.16	3.16	1	.075	0.75
Education	1.19	0.74	2.59	1	.108	3.28
Project size	0.98	0.78	1.57	1	.210	2.66
Software	-0.36	1.01	0.13	1	.723	0.70
Hardware	2.35	0.98	5.74	1	.017	10.47
Services	-1.39	0.72	3.67	1	.055	0.25
Other	0.22	1.39	0.02	1	.876	1.24
Duration	0.33	0.66	0.25	1	.618	1.39
Schedule						
Experience	-0.14	0.22	0.38	1	.540	0.87
Certi-fication	-0.29	0.17	3.02	1	.082	0.75
Education	-0.71	0.65	1.19	1	.276	0.49
Project size	0.16	0.72	0.05	1	.819	1.18
Software	0.25	0.87	0.08	1	.777	1.28
Hardware	0.52	0.74	0.50	1	.482	1.68

Source	B	SE	Wald	df	p	OR
Services	-1.12	0.64	3.10	1	.078	0.33
Other	0.35	1.31	0.07	1	.789	1.42
Duration	0.43	0.65	0.45	1	.504	1.54
Scope						
Experience	0.37	0.24	2.29	1	.130	1.44
Certifi-cation	-0.25	0.16	2.62	1	.105	0.78
Education	1.23	0.82	2.24	1	.135	3.40
Project size	0.38	0.82	0.21	1	.646	1.46
Software	0.00	0.99	0.00	1	.997	1.00
Hardware	-0.15	0.74	0.04	1	.845	0.87
Services	-1.00	0.69	2.09	1	.148	0.37
Other	-0.68	1.26	0.29	1	.590	0.51
Duration	-0.57	0.72	0.62	1	.433	0.57

Note. Budget: $\chi^2(9) = 11.96$, $p = .215$, Nagelkerke $R^2 = .21$. Schedule: $\chi^2(9) = 11.21$, $p = .262$, Nagelkerke $R^2 = .19$. Scope: $\chi^2(9) = 14.79$, $p = .097$, Nagelkerke $R^2 = .26$.

The first logistic regression was conducted on budget, and the results were not statistically significant, $\chi^2(9) = 11.96$, $p = .215$, Nagelkerke $R^2 = .21$, suggesting that experience, certification, education, project size, type, and duration could not predict if the IT project would be completed within budget. No statistical significance exists.

The second logistic regression was conducted on schedule, and the results were not statistically significant, $\chi^2(9) = 11.21$, $p = .262$, Nagelkerke $R^2 = .19$, suggesting that experience, certification, education, project size, type, and duration could not predict if the IT project would be completed within schedule (0 = more than 15% under/more than 15% over vs. 1 = within 15% of original/no variance). No statistical significance exists.

The third logistic regression was conducted on scope, and the results were not statistically significant, $\chi^2(9) = 14.79$, $p = .097$, Nagelkerke $R^2 = .26$, suggesting that experience, certification, education, project size, type, and duration could not predict if the IT project would be completed within scope. No statistical significance exists. The null hypothesis – there is no statistical relationship between reported project success and project manager experience, certification, level of education, and project size, type, and duration – cannot be rejected.

Research Question 3

Research Question 3 asked, Does the utilization of project risk management processes correlate with project success more than project manager experience, certification, level of education, and project size, type, or duration?

To address Research Question 3, three chi-square difference tests were conducted to determine if there are significant differences between the chi-square models found in Research Questions 1 and 2. One difference test was conducted for each dependent variable used in Research Questions 1 and 2: budget, schedule, and scope. Statistical significance was determined at $\alpha = .05$. The results of the chi-square difference tests are presented in Table 7.

Table 7. Chi-Square Difference Tests on Budget, Schedule, and Scope

Variable	Research Question 2		Research Question 1		Difference		
	x^2	df	x^2	df	x^2	df	p
Budget	11.96	9	4.74	6	7.22	3	.065
Schedule	11.21	9	1.07	6	10.14	3	.017
Scope	14.79	9	5.54	6	9.25	3	.026

The first chi-square difference test was conducted on budget, and the results were not statistically significant, $x^2(3) = 7.22$, $p = .065$, suggesting the chi-square model from Research Question 1 is not statistically different from the chi-square model found from Research Question 2 on budget. No statistical significance exists.

The second chi-square difference test was conducted on schedule, and the results were statistically significant, $\chi^2(3) = 10.14$, $p = .017$, suggesting the chi-square model from Research Question 1 is statistically different from the chi-square model found from Research Question 2 on schedule. Because neither model significantly predicted schedule, the difference exists.

The third chi-square difference test was conducted on scope, and the results were statistically significant, $\chi^2(3) = 9.25$, $p = .026$, indicating the chi-square model from Research Question 1 is statistically different from the chi-square model found from Research Question 2 on scope. Because neither model significantly predicted scope, the difference cannot be interpreted. The null hypothesis - there is no statistical relationship between the utilization of project risk management processes with project success more than project manager experience, certification, level of education, and project size, type, or duration – cannot be rejected.

CHAPTER 5. DISCUSSION

Introduction

Chapter 5 provides a summary and discussion of the study's results, implications, limitations, and recommendations for further research. The Summary of the Results section briefly reviews the original research question and subsidiary research questions as compared to the study's findings. In the Discussion of the Results section, an interpretation of the study is presented. The Implications of the Study Results section relates notable findings to project management professionals and stakeholders alike. The limitations of the study are followed by recommendations for further research.

The purpose of this study was to gain an understanding of whether utilizing project risk management processes correlated with improved IT project success as measured by self-reported variance in planned versus actual end-of-project budget, schedule, and scope. This is in light of increasingly complex projects that place a reward on risk analysis (Laufer et al., 1996). Due to project management practitioners' typically limited time and resources, elucidating positive evidence of the benefit in using these tools and techniques is of utmost importance (de Bakker et al., 2009). Tying theory to practice, namely, the principles of simultaneous management, knowledge-dependent outcomes, and time-bound constraints as espoused by Laufer et al. (1996), it is clear that in the context of project management, there is no such thing as one size fits all. With that said, contingency theory (Shenhar & Dvir, 2007) makes the argument that adaptation, particularly around the topic of risk management, enables the creation of strategic value. Coming full circle, utilization of project risk management processes may indeed represent a shift in practice, which ultimately could demonstrate both feasible and incremental value to organizations that are proponents of increasing IT project value.

Summary of the Results

The quantitative study used 78 survey responses to serve as the statistical basis of findings and subsequent interpretation of results. Of the 171 surveys sent, 107 were determined to meet the study requirements, and of those that qualified, 78 were completed in full. The survey instrument consisted of 24 multiple-choice questions and was piloted prior to release to qualified study participants. The survey included demographic questions in addition to questions based on the participant's self-reported use of specific project risk management tools and techniques on a recently completed project selected at the start of the survey.

Research Question 1 asked, to what extent is utilization of project risk management processes (planning, identifying, qualitative, quantitative, responding, and controlling) related to project success outcomes (budget, schedule, and scope)? The results of logistic regression analyses suggested use of project risk management processes did not predict project success outcomes.

Research Question 2 asked, what is the correlation between reported project success and project manager experience, certification, level of education, and project size, type, and duration? The results of the logistic regression analysis suggested that experience, certification, education, project size, type, and duration did not predict project success outcomes.

Research Question 3 asked, Does the utilization of project risk management processes correlate with project success more than project manager experience, certification, level of education, and project size, type, or duration? The results of the chi-square difference tests suggested the utilization of project risk management processes did correlate with project success more than project manager experience, certification, level of education, and project size, type, or duration when evaluating project success outcomes in terms of schedule and scope, but not budget.

To gain additional insight into the data, Spearman correlations were conducted between variables of interest, including those not directly tied to the principle or subsidiary research questions. A significant, negative correlation was found between a project manager's experience in terms of years and the number of project management qualifications held, IT projects that involved hardware, and all five project risk management processes. On the other hand, positive relationships were found between the number of qualifications the project manager held, IT projects that involved hardware, and all five project risk management processes.

Project size in terms of the number of people dedicated to the IT project was positively related to IT projects that involved services, the duration of the IT project, identifying project risk management processes, qualitative project risk management processes, and quantitative project risk management processes. IT projects that involved software were negatively related to IT projects that involved services in addition to the IT project category of "other."

IT projects that involved hardware were positively related to planning project risk management processes, quantitative project risk management processes, and responding project risk management processes. Duration of the IT project was positively related to qualitative project risk management processes and quantitative project risk management processes. Lastly, all five project risk management processes were positively related to the other project risk management processes examined in the study.

Discussion of the Results

While the results of the study did not show correlation within the use of project risk management processes or project manager experience, certification, level of education, and project size, type, or duration with project success, results demonstrated there could be a correlation between the use of project risk management processes more than project manager experience, certification, level of education, and project size, type, or duration when considering project schedule and scope success metrics, which was a significant finding. Because the study models failed to fully predict project success in all categories tested, the null hypotheses could not be rejected for any of the original research questions.

In taking a positivist epistemological stance, the researcher sought to uncover, through evidence-based management, specific cause-and-effect type relationships. A statistical correlation was indicated between the use of project risk management processes and IT project success. The implications for managers, companies, and stakeholders of IT projects, as the evidence indicates, is the observation that use of project risk management processes relates to IT project success, particularly when IT projects were measured in terms of being delivered on time and within scope.

Based on a review of the literature, it was not a surprise that a correlation between use of project risk management tools and project success could be measured at a high level. PMI (2009) argued the use of project risk management tools and techniques help to increase the likelihood of positive events and decrease the impact of negative events. Similarly, Raz et al. (2002) were able to link process success with use of risk management practices that aimed to control uncertainty. Cooke-Davies (2002) found four out of 12 factors affecting progress success could be linked to risk management. From a strategic management view, use of project risk management was found to be worthwhile for 75% of those surveyed.

What was surprising was the study failed to relate specific project risk management tools and techniques to project success as measured by the responses recorded in the survey instrument. The survey was developed by close examination of the literature and subcategorized the questions into the project risk management process groups (a) planning; (b) identifying; (c) analyzing, both qualitative and quantitative types; (d) responding; and (e) controlling. The lack of correlation was in sharp contrast to the evidence found within literature reviewed in each of these areas.

For example, within the project risk management process group of plan risk management, previous researchers found defining success factors (Mazouz et al., 2008; PMI, 2009; Ward, 1999b), tailoring risk management to projects (Boehm, 1991; Flyvbjerg, 2006; Meier, 2008; Rosacker & Olson, 2008), assessing risk thresholds (Asnar & Zannone, 2008; Huff & Prybutok, 2008; Islam, 2009), communicating effectively (Csiszar, 2008; Hinrichs, 2009; Mikes, 2009), and managing stakeholder expectations (Bourne & Walker, 2006; Brook, 2005; Mazouz et al., 2008) were common to the process group.

Within the project risk management process group of identify risks, previous researchers found that risk categorization (Chatzoglou & Diamantidis, 2009; Warkentin et al., 2009), risk ownership (Addison, 2003; Busby & Zhang, 2008; Du et al., 2007; Hubbard, 2009; Pavlak, 2004; Raz et al., 2002), use of a risk register (Cooke-Davies, 2002; Krane et al., 2010; Reich, 2007; Sanchez et al., 2008; Ward, 1999a; Williams, 1997), and integrating risk identification (Boehm, 1991; Kajko-Mattsson, 2009; Raz & Michael, 2001; Royer, 2000) were common to the process group.

Within the project risk management process group of perform qualitative risk analysis, previous researchers found measuring probability and impact (Hillson, 2009; Mulcahy, 2010; Pyra & Trask, 2002; Ward, 1999a) was fundamental to the process group.

Within the project risk management process group of perform quantitative risk analysis, previous researchers found the use of numerical models (Dunkel & Weber, 2007; Jackson & Al-Hamdani, 2008; McLain, 2009; Miranda & Abran, 2008; Pollack-Johnson & Liberatore, 2005; Regev et al., 2006; Voetsch et al., 2004) and assessment of risk combinatorial effects (Baccarini & Archer, 2001; Hillson, 2009) were common to the process group.

Within the project risk management process group of plan risk response, previous researchers found use of strategy (Addison & Vallabh, 2002; Hillson, 2009; Mulcahy, 2010; Rush & Vednere, 2008), risk register updates (Mulcahy, 2010), assignment of action owners (Hinrichs, 2009; Raz et al., 2002), project management plan updates (Bark et al., 2001; Ben-David & Raz, 2001), and reassessment of success factors (Boehm, 1991; Keil et al., 1998) were common to the process group.

Finally, within the project risk management process group of monitor and control risk, previous researchers found tracking (Boehm, 1991; PMI, 2009), reporting (Hillson, 2009), assessment of organizational processes (Mulcahy, 2010; Voetsch et al., 2004), communication (Mulcahy, 2010), and observation

(Freimut et al., 2001; Ingley & Walt, 2008; Kontio et al., 1998; Raz & Michael, 2001) were common to the process group.

While the results of the study were unexpected, several factors could be at play, namely, the newness of the survey instrument and lack of maturity within the practice of project risk management. Kutsch and Hall (2009), for example, stated nearly one-third of project managers do not use formal project risk management processes. If the IT project managers surveyed used informal project risk management processes, which were not measured, the study results could be skewed. In this regard, since the survey instrument itself was new, a better job could be done to refine the questions to capture both specific and general project risk management practices.

Overall, the preponderance of literature in the relatively new field of formalized project risk management, in face of some of the study's results, should not dissuade the reader in thinking there is little value in its practice. On the other hand, the field is ripe for further study and inquiry, as Implications of the study results show.

Implications of the Study Results

The study found statistically significant predictors of project success when considering the use of project risk management processes over a project manager's experience or IT project composition in a majority of the categories measured. What this means is if Research Question 3 were broken down into discrete sub-questions, the null hypothesis for each could have been rejected in the cases involving schedule and scope. Gaining insight into the relationship between the use of project risk management and project success, as the study revealed, suggests a renewed sense of urgency to the thoughtful examination on the topic and of the measured positive impact that use of these tools has on IT projects overall. Similar to how Raz et al. (2002) linked project success with risk management and the control of uncertainty, further implications from this study involve communicating how project risk management processes may positively influence projects. This communication, as evidenced by the high-level results, may help to sway stakeholders averse to the investment of project risk management tools and techniques as a whole.

As the results revealed utilization of project risk management tools and techniques better predicted project success when looking at schedule and scope, than of project manger's experience, project size, type, or duration, the argument could be made organizations, sponsors, and stakeholders should insist on utilization of project risk management tools and techniques, especially in cases where projects are constrained by time or when high-quality results matter most (de Bakker et al., 2009). What is anticipated is a thoughtful examination and evaluation of existing project management tools and techniques as compared and contrasted to those of IT project end goals. While results of this study did not indicate any specific project risk management tool or technique is more useful than another, the researcher believed this did not negate the need to use project risk management processes as a general best practice. The literature and findings of this study showed two commonalities: (a) not all IT projects are successful and (b) not all IT projects use project risk management processes. Extrapolating from both data and literature, implications of the study make it clear time and effort would not be wasted in the pursuit of factors, including the use of project risk management tools and techniques, that positively impact project success.

Limitations

Limitations included a smaller-than-expected sample size and survey participant demographics skewing to those with fewer project management-based qualifications. These limitations could have been related to the pool of project managers recruited for the study and the lack of screening for project managers who had less experience managing IT projects than others. If the study were to be repeated, a greater recruitment effort could lead to increased statistical relevance for the greater population of IT project managers.

The survey instrument itself could be improved. The instrument was newly created for the study, so an opportunity exists for additional internal and external validity efforts. The instrument focused mainly on project risk management tools and techniques. It did not control for other project management practices that may also contribute to project success. By limiting the instrument, additional valuable data could have been excluded and tested, namely, non-project risk management factors that may affect project success. Addressing these limitations would enable the study to describe, explain, predict, and control for project success.

Recommendations for Further Research

As the study showed, research opportunities in the area of both project risk management and other factors that affect project success abound. Whether addressing the current limitations or exploring additional areas as supported by both theory and previous studies, the body of knowledge on this important topic can be further expanded. For example, conducting further analysis of common project risk management tools or techniques associated with differing levels of project success, whether they are related to project risk management or other project management processes, could bring additional and valuable findings to light.

It would be thought-provoking to explore, for example, if other project management processes affect project success more than project risk management processes. Other areas to investigate include the project risk management processes used less often or not at all compared to others, as related to a project manager's training, education, or experience. Additional modifications to the study could include asking different questions on what constitutes project success other than the measures asked specific to budget, schedule, and scope variance.

Even with the survey data collected, the opportunity exists to explore additional statistical tests and analyses. The basis of these analyses could lead to additional findings not asked in the original research questions, such as if project managers with more experience used certain tools and techniques more successfully than those with less experience, and how that impacted project success. It could be valuable to study the effect of a project's size, duration, or cost, independent of tools and techniques used. These findings would be compared to project success and, lastly, whether project success is partially or fully subjective to the perspective of the project manager, project sponsor, or end user of the IT project.

REFERENCES

Addison, T. (2003). E-commerce project development risks: Evidence from a Delphi survey. *International Journal of Information Management, 23*(1), 25–40. doi:10 .1016/S0268-4012(02)00066-X

Addison, T., & Vallabh, S. (2002, September). *Controlling software project risks: An empirical study of methods used by experienced project managers.* Paper presented at the annual research conference of the South African Institute of Computer Scientists and Information Technologists on Enablement Through Technology, Port Elizabeth, South Africa. Retrieved from http://dl.acm.org /citation.cfm?id=581506.581525

Asnar, Y., & Zannone, N. (2008, October). *Perceived risk assessment.* Paper presented at the 4th ACM workshop on Quality of Protection, Alexandria, VA. doi:10.1145 /1456362.1456375

Aubert, B. A., Patry, M., & Rivard, S. (2005). A framework for information technology outsourcing risk management. *SIGMIS Database, 36*(4), 9–28. doi:10.1145 /1104004.1104007

Baccarini, D., & Archer, R. (2001). The risk ranking of projects: A methodology. *International Journal of Project Management, 19*(3), 139–145. doi:10.1016 /S0263-7863(99)00074-5

Barki, H., Rivard, S., & Talbot, J. (2001). An integrative contingency model of software project risk management. *Journal of Management Information Systems, 17*(4), 37–69. Retrieved from http://mesharpe.metapress.com/link.asp?id =ycfeqct9tvxnkdt9

Ben-David, I., & Raz, T. (2001). An integrated approach for risk response development in project planning. *Journal of the Operational Research Society, 52*(1), 14. Retrieved from http://www.jstor.org/stable/254104

Boehm, B. W. (1991, January/February). Software risk management: Principles and practices. *IEEE Software, 8*(1), 32–41. doi:10.1109/52.62930

Bourne, L., & Walker, D. H. T. (2006). Visualizing stakeholder influence: Two Australian examples. *Project Management Journal, 37*(1), 5–21. Retrieved from http://www.pmi.org/Knowledge-Center/Publications-Online-Library/PMJ-Past -Issues.aspx

Brook, G. (2005). Surviving the roller coaster: Worst practices in project management within the television production industry. *Project Management Journal, 36*(1), 5–14. Retrieved from http://www.pmi.org/Knowledge-Center/Publications-Online -Library/PMJ-Past-Issues.aspx

Busby, J. S., & Zhang, H. (2008). The pathogen construct in risk analysis. *Project Management Journal, 39*(3), 86–96. Retrieved from http://www.pmi.org/Knowledge-Center/Publications-Online-Library/PMJ-Past -Issues.aspx

Chatzoglou, P. D., & Diamantidis, A. D. (2009). IT/IS implementation risks and their impact on firm performance. *International Journal of Information Management, 29*(2), 119–128. doi:10.1016/j.ijinfomgt.2008.04.008

Cooke-Davies, T. (2002). The "real" success factors on projects. *International Journal of Project Management, 20*(3), 185–190. doi:10.1016/S0263-7863(01)00067-9

Cooper, D. R., & Schindler, P. S. (2006). *Business research methods* (9th ed.). New York, NY: McGraw-Hill Irwin.

Cox, L. A., Jr. (2008). What's wrong with risk matrices? *Risk Analysis: An International Journal, 28*(2), 497–512. doi:10.1111/j.1539-6924.2008.01030.x

Csiszar, E. N. (2008). Managing risk and uncertainty. *Business & Economic Review, 55*(1), 3–7. Retrieved from http://www.scinsnews.com/resources/Csiszar_article .pdf

de Bakker, K., Boonstra, A., & Wortmann, H. (2009). Does risk management contribute to IT project success? A meta-analysis of empirical evidence. *International Journal of Project Management, 28*(5), 493–503. doi:10.1016/j.ijproman.2009.07 .002

Dimitroff, R. D., Schmidt, L. A., & Bond, T. D. (2005). Organizational behavior and disaster: A study of conflict at NASA. *Project Management Journal, 36*(2), 28–38. Retrieved from http://www.pmi.org/Knowledge-Center/Publications-Online -Library/PMJ-Past-Issues.aspx

Du, S., Keil, M., Mathiassen, L., Shen, Y., & Tiwana, A. (2007). Attention-shaping tools, expertise, and perceived control in IT project risk assessment. *Decision Support Systems, 43*(1), 269–283. doi:10.1016/j.dss.2006.10.002

Dunkel, J., & Weber, S. (2007, December). *Efficient Monte Carlo methods for convex risk measures in portfolio credit risk models.* Paper presented at the 39th conference on Winter Simulation: 40 Years! The Best Is Yet to Come, Washington DC. doi:10.1109/WSC.2007.4419692

Flyvbjerg, B. (2006). From Nobel prize to project management: Getting risks right. *Project Management Journal, 37*(3), 5–15. Retrieved from http://www.pmi.org /Knowledge-Center/Publications-Online-Library/PMJ-Past-Issues.aspx

Fowler, F. J. (2002). *Survey research methods* (3rd ed.). Thousand Oaks, CA: Sage.

Freeman, M., & Beale, P. (1992). Measuring project success. *Project Management Journal, 23*(1), 8-17. Retrieved from http://marketplace.pmi.org/Pages /ProductDetail.aspx?GMProduct=00100690000&iss=1

Freimut, B., Hartkopf, S., Kaiser, P., Kontio, J., & Kobitzsch, W. (2001, September). *An industrial case study of implementing software risk management.* Paper presented at the 8th European Software Engineering Conference held jointly with 9th ACM SIGSOFT International Symposium on Foundations of Software Engineering, Vienna, Austria. doi:10.1145/503271.503247

George, D., & Mallery, P. (2010). *SPSS for Windows step by step: A simple guide and reference, 18.0 update* (11th ed.). Boston, MA: Allyn & Bacon.

Hillson, D. (2002). Extending the risk process to manage opportunities. *International Journal of Project Management, 20*(3), 235–240. doi:10.1016/S0263-7863(01)00074-6

Hillson, D. (2009). *Managing risk in projects.* Burlington, England: Gower.

Hinrichs, J. (2009). Creating synergy by integrating enterprise risk management and governance. *Journal of Risk Management in Financial Institutions, 2*(2), 155–164. Retrieved from http://henrystewart.metapress.com/link.asp?id =448lh45202561r52

Hubbard, L. (2009). The matrix revisited. *Internal Auditor, 66*(2), 55–57. Retrieved from http://ezproxy.library.capella.edu/login?url=http://search.ebscoh ost.com/login .aspx?direct=true&db=bth&AN=14038171&site=ehost-live&scope=site

Huff, R. A., & Prybutok, V. R. (2008). Information systems project management decision making: The influence of experience and risk propensity. *Project Management Journal, 39*(2), 34–47.

Retrieved from http://www.pmi.org/Knowledge-Center /Publications-Online-Library/PMJ-Past-Issues.aspx

Ingley, C., & Walt, N. V. (2008). Risk management and board effectiveness. *International Studies of Management & Organization, 38*(3), 43–70. Retrieved from http://mesharpe.metapress.com/link.asp?id=e02m3l038185q2h 6

Islam, S. (2009, August). *Software development risk management model: A goal driven approach.* Paper presented at the doctoral symposium for ESEC/FSE, Amsterdam, Netherlands. doi:10.1145/1595782.1595785

Jackson, L. A., & Al-Hamdani, W. (2008, September). *Economic acceptable risk assessment model.* Paper presented at the 5th annual conference on Information Security Curriculum Development, Kennesaw, GA. doi:10.1145/1456625 .1456636

Kajko-Mattsson, M. (2009, November). Laying out the scope of developers' risk management responsibilities. *Proceedings of the 2nd International Conference on Interaction Sciences: Information Technology, Culture and Human, 230-235.* doi: 10.1145/1655925.1655966

Keil, M., Cule, P. E., Lyytinen, K., & Schmidt, R. C. (1998). A framework for identifying software project risks. *Communications of the ACM, 41*(11), 76–83. doi:10.1145/287831.287843

Kendrick, T. (2009). *Identifying and managing project risk* (2nd ed.). New York, NY: American Management Association.

Kerzner, H. (2009). *Project management: A systems approach to planning, scheduling, and controlling* (10th ed.). Hoboken, NJ: Wiley.

Kontio, J., Getto, G., & Landes, D. (1998, November). *Experiences in improving risk management processes using the concepts of the Riskit method.* Paper presented at the 6th ACM SIGSOFT international symposium on Foundations of Software Engineering, Lake Buena Vista, FL. doi:10.1145/288195.288301

Krane, H., Rolstadås, A., & Olsson, N. (2010). Categorizing risks in seven large projects: Which risks do the projects focus on? *Project Management Journal, 41*(1), 81. Retrieved from http://www.pmi.org/Knowledge-Center/Publications-Online -Library/PMJ-Past-Issues.aspx

Kutsch, E., & Hall, M. (2009). The rational choice of not applying project risk management in information technology projects. *Project Management Journal, 40*(3), 72. Retrieved from http://www.pmi.org/Knowledge-Center/Publications

-Online-Library/PMJ-Past-Issues.aspx

Kwak, Y. H., & Anbari, F. T. (2009). Analyzing project management research: Perspectives from top management journals. *International Journal of Project Management, 27*(5), 435–446. doi:10.1016/j.ijproman.2008.08.004

Laufer, A., Denker, G. R., & Shenhar, A. J. (1996). Simultaneous management: The key to excellence in capital projects. *International Journal of Project Management, 14*(4), 189–199. doi:10.1016/0263-7863(95)00091-7

Mazouz, B., Facal, J., & Viola, J.-M. (2008). Public–private partnership: Elements for a project-based management typology. *Project Management Journal, 39*(2), 98–110. Retrieved from http://www.pmi.org/Knowledge-Center/Publications-Online -Library/PMJ-Past-Issues.aspx

McCray, G. E., Purvis, R. L., & McCray, C. G. (2002). Project management under uncertainty: The impact of heuristics and biases. *Project Management Journal, 33*(1), 49-57. Retrieved from http://marketplace.pmi.org/Pages/ProductDetail .aspx?GMProduct=00100248200&iss=1

McLain, D. (2009). Quantifying project characteristics related to uncertainty. *Project Management Journal, 40*(4), 60. Retrieved from http://www.pmi.org/Knowledge -Center/Publications-Online-Library/PMJ-Past-Issues.aspx

Meier, S. R. (2008). Best project management and systems engineering practices in the preacquisition phase for federal intelligence and defense agencies. *Project Management Journal, 39*(1), 59–71. Retrieved from http://www.pmi.org /Knowledge-Center/Publications-Online-Library/PMJ-Past-Issues.aspx

Mikes, A. (2009). Risk management and calculative cultures. *Management Accounting Research, 20*(1), 18–40. doi:10.1016/j.mar.2008.10.005

Miranda, E., & Abran, A. (2008). Protecting software development projects against underestimation. *Project Management Journal, 39*(3), 75–85. Retrieved from http://www.pmi.org/Knowledge-Center/Publications-Online-Library/PMJ-Past -Issues.aspx

Morris, P. W. G., & Jamieson, A. (2005). Moving from corporate strategy to project strategy. *Project Management Journal, 36*(4), 5–18. Retrieved from http://www .pmi.org/Knowledge-Center/Publications-Online-Library/PMJ-Past-Issues.aspx

Mulcahy, R. (2010). *Risk management tricks of the trade for project managers* (2nd ed.). Minnetonka, MN: RMC.

Padayachee, K. (2002, September). *An interpretive study of software risk management perspectives.* Paper presented at the annual research conference of the South African Institute of Computer Scientists and Information Technologists on Enablement Through Technology, Port Elizabeth, South Africa. Retrieved from http://dl.acm.org/citation.cfm?id=581524

Pavlak, A. (2004). Project troubleshooting: Tiger teams for reactive risk management. *Project Management Journal, 35*(4), 5–14. Retrieved from http://marketplace.pmi .org/Pages/ProductDetail.aspx?GMProduct=00100826500&iss= 1

Perminova, O., Gustafsson, M., & Wikström, K. (2007). Defining uncertainty in projects: A new perspective. *International Journal of Project Management, 26*(1), 73–79. doi:10.1016/j.ijproman.2007.08.005

Pinto, J. K., & Slevin, D. P. (1988). Project success: Definitions and measurement techniques. *Project Management Journal, 19*(1), 67-72. Retrieved from http:// marketplace.pmi.org/Pages/ProductDetail.aspx?GMProduct=00 100879500&iss=1

Pollack-Johnson, B., & Liberatore, M. J. (2005). Project planning under uncertainty using scenario analysis. *Project Management Journal, 36*(1), 15–26. Retrieved from http://www.pmi.org/Knowledge-Center/Publications-Online-Library/PMJ-Past -Issues.aspx

Project Management Institute. (2008). *A guide to the project management body of knowledge* (4th ed.). Newtown Square, PA: Author.

Project Management Institute. (2009). *Practice standard for project risk management.* Newtown Square, PA: Author.

Pyra, J., & Trask, J. (2002). Risk management post analysis: Gauging the success of a simple strategy in a complex project. *Project Management Journal, 33*(2), 41. Retrieved from http://marketplace.pmi.org/Pages/ProductDetail.aspx?GMProdu ct =00100352900&iss=1

Raz, T., & Michael, E. (2001). Use and benefits of tools for project risk management. *International Journal of Project Management, 19*(1), 9–17. doi:10.1016/S0263 -7863(99)00036-8

Raz, T., Shenhar, A. J., & Dvir, D. (2002). Risk management, project success, and technological uncertainty. *R&D Management, 32*(2), 101. doi:10.1111/1467-9310 .00243

Regev, S., Shtub, A., & Ben-Haim, Y. (2006). Managing project risks as knowledge gaps. *Project Management Journal, 37*(5), 17–25. Retrieved from http://www.pmi .org/Knowledge-Center/Publications-Online-Library/PMJ-Past-Issues.aspx

Reich, B. H. (2007). Managing knowledge and learning in IT projects: A conceptual framework and guidelines for practice. *Project Management Journal, 38*(2), 5–17. Retrieved from http://www.pmi.org/Knowledge-Center/Publications-Online -Library/PMJ-Past-Issues.aspx

Rosacker, K. M., & Olson, D. L. (2008). An empirical assessment of IT project selection and evaluation methods in state government. *Project Management Journal, 39*(1), 49–58. Retrieved from http://www.pmi.org/Knowledge-Center/Publications -Online-Library/PMJ-Past-Issues.aspx

Royer, P. S. (2000). Risk management: The undiscovered dimension of project management. *Project Management Journal, 31*(1), 6. Retrieved from http:// marketplace.pmi.org/Pages/ProductDetail.aspx?GMProduct=00 100278900&iss=1

Rush, M., & Vednere, G. (2008). Calming the data storm: A risk management model for mitigating risks. *Information Management Journal, 42*(4), 48. Available from ProQuest Dissertations and Theses database. (UMI No. 227758320)

Sanchez, H., Robert, B., & Pellerin, R. (2008). A project portfolio risk–opportunity identification framework. *Project Management Journal, 39*(3), 97–109. Retrieved from http://www.pmi.org/Knowledge-Center/Publications-Online-Library/PMJ -Past-Issues.aspx

Shenhar, A. J. (2001). One size does not fit all projects: Exploring classical contingency domains. *Management Science, 47*(3), 394. doi:10.1287/mnsc.47.3.394.9772

Shenhar, A. J., & Dvir, D. (1996). Toward a typological theory of project management. *Research Policy, 25*(4), 607–632. doi:10.1016/0048-7333(95)00877-2

Shenhar, A. J., & Dvir, D. (2007). Project management research— The challenge and opportunity. *Project Management Journal, 38*(2), 93. Retrieved from http://www .pmi.org/Knowledge-Center/Publications-Online-Library/PMJ-Past-Issues.aspx

Söderlund, J. (2004). Building theories of project management: Past research, questions for the future. *International Journal of Project Management, 22*(3), 183–191. doi:

10.1016/S0263-7863(03)00070-X

Taylor, H. (2006). Risk management and problem resolution strategies for IT projects: Prescription and practice. *Project Management Journal, 37*(5), 49–63. Retrieved from http://www.pmi.org/Knowledge-Center/Publications-Online-Library/PMJ
-Past-Issues.aspx

Voetsch, R., Cioffi, D., & Anbari, F. (2004, August). *Project risk management practices and their association with reported project success.* Paper presented at the International Research Network on Organizing by Projects (IRNOP VI), Turku, Finland. Retrieved from http://marcoullis.com/PROJECTS/ANBARI/pdf/selected /Anbari_Research_PROJECT_RISK_MANAGEMENT_PRACTI CES.pdf

Wallace, L., & Keil, M. (2004). Software project risks and their effect on outcomes. *Communications of the ACM, 47*(4), 68–73. doi:10.1145/975817.975819

Ward, S. (1999a). Assessing and managing important risks. *International Journal of Project Management, 17*(6), 331–336. doi:10.1016/S0263-7863(98)00051-9

Ward, S. (1999b). Requirements for an effective project risk management process. *Project Management Journal, 30*(3), 37. Retrieved from http://marketplace.pmi .org/Pages/ProductDetail.aspx?GMProduct=00100197900

Warkentin, M., Moore, R. S., Bekkering, E., & Johnston, A. C. (2009). Analysis of systems development project risks: An integrative framework. *SIGMIS Database, 40*(2), 8–27. doi:10.1145/1531817.1531821

Williams, T. M. (1996). The two-dimensionality of project risk. *International Journal of Project Management, 14*(3), 185–186. doi:10.1016/0263-7863(96)00030-0

Williams, T. M. (1997). Empowerment vs. risk management? *International Journal of Project Management, 15*(4), 219–222. doi:10.1016/S0263-7863(96)00074-9

APPENDIX

SURVEY INSTRUMENT

Please answer the following questions about yourself and experience.

1. Select which best fits your most recent IT project job function or title.
   ☐ Project Manager
   ☐ Project Coordinator
   ☐ Project Analyst
   ☐ Project Leader
   ☐ Other

2. For your last IT project assignment, what was your job status?
   ☐ Contractor
   ☐ Employee
   ☐ Other

3. Describe the amount of time you spent managing IT projects when you had this responsibility.
   ☐ Up to half time
   ☐ More than half time but less than full time
   ☐ Full time

4. Identify your primary work location in addition to employer and customer location.

	North America, United States	Europe, Africa, Middle East	Asia, Pacific	Latin America	Other
Work location	☐	☐	☐	☐	☐
Employer location	☐	☐	☐	☐	☐
Customer location	☐	☐	☐	☐	☐

5. Which industry best describes the company's focus at your current or last place of employment, in which you recently completed an IT project?
   ☐ Advertising, Marketing
   ☐ Airlines, Aerospace, Defense
   ☐ Automotive
   ☐ Construction
   ☐ Education
   ☐ Entertainment
   ☐ Financial Services
   ☐ Food, Beverages
   ☐ Government
   ☐ Health Care, Pharmaceuticals
   ☐ Information Technology
   ☐ Insurance
   ☐ Nonprofit
   ☐ Retail, Consumer, Electronics
   ☐ Utilities, Energy

6. Please mark from the following which qualification(s) or certification(s) you have earned.

☐ American Academy of Project Management (AAPM)
☐ Capability Maturity Model Integration (CMMI)
☐ Certificate in Project Management
☐ Certificate in Risk Management
☐ Certified Associate in Project Management (CAPM)
☐ Information Technology Infrastructure Library (ITIL)
☐ Lean Six Sigma
☐ PMI Agile Certified Practitioner (PMI-ACP)
☐ PMI Risk Management Professional (PMI-RMP)
☐ PMI Scheduling Professional (PMI-SP)
☐ Program Management Professional (PgMP)
☐ Project Management Professional (PMP)
☐ Comp TIA Project+
☐ Projects in Controlled Environments (PRINCE2)
☐ Six Sigma Black Belt
☐ Six Sigma Green Belt
☐ None of the above

7. Please indicate the number of years of experience you have in the following areas.

	Up to 2 years	More than 2 and up to 4 years	More than 4 and up to 6 years	More than 6 and up to 8 years	More than 8 years	None
IT project management	☐	☐	☐	☐	☐	☐
IT project risk management	☐	☐	☐	☐	☐	☐
Resource management	☐	☐	☐	☐	☐	☐

	Up to 2 years	More than 2 and up to 4 years	More than 4 and up to 6 years	More than 6 and up to 8 years	More than 8 years	None
Technical management	☐	☐	☐	☐	☐	☐

8. Please indicate the highest level college degree, if any, successfully completed.

   ☐ No degree
   ☐ Associate's degree
   ☐ Bachelor's degree
   ☐ Master's degree
   ☐ Doctoral degree

Select a single IT project that you recently completed in order to answer this and all remaining survey questions.

9. How long ago did the IT project you selected finish?
   ☐ Finished within the last 2 years
   ☐ Finished more than 2 years ago

10. How many people dedicated at least half their time to the IT project?
   ☐ Up to 4 people
   ☐ 5-10 people
   ☐ 11-20 people
   ☐ More than 20 people

11. What was the total duration of the IT project?
   ☐ Up to 3 months
   ☐ More than 3 months but less than 6 months
   ☐ More than 6 months but less than 12 months
   ☐ More than 12 months

12. What was the total cost for the IT project in US Dollars (USD)?

   ☐ Up to $100,000
   ☐ More than $100,000 but less than $500,000
   ☐ More than $500,000 but less than $1,000,000
   ☐ More than $1,000,000

13. Describe the size of your employer and the size of the target customer base for this IT project.

	Up to 100 people	100-500 people	501-1,000 people	1,001-5,000 people	5,001-10,000 people	More than 10,000 people
Employer	☐	☐	☐	☐	☐	☐
Customer base	☐	☐	☐	☐	☐	☐

14. Which of the following categories describes the type of IT project you worked on?
   ☐ Software
   ☐ Hardware
   ☐ Services
   ☐ Other

For the same IT project you selected, please respond to the project success questions listed below.

15. Describe the final end of the project variance, if any, to the IT project.

	More than 15% under original	Within 15% of original	More than 15% over original plan	No variance
Variance in planned versus actual scope (in terms of deliverables)	☐	☐	☐	☐
Variance in planned versus actual schedule (in terms of duration)	☐	☐	☐	☐
Variance in planned versus actual budget (in terms of cost)	☐	☐	☐	☐

16. Describe the negative impact the variance had, if any, to the IT project.

	No Impact	Low Impact	Below average impact	Average impact	Above average impact	High impact	N/A
Difference in planned versus actual scope (in terms of deliverables)	☐	☐	☐	☐	☐	☐	☐
Difference in planned	☐	☐	☐	☐	☐	☐	☐

	No Impact	Low Impact	Below average impact	Average impact	Above average impact	High impact	N/A
versus actual schedule (in terms of duration)							
Difference in planned versus actual budget (in terms of cost)	☐	☐	☐	☐	☐	☐	☐

17. Please select the final status of the IT project from the following perspectives.

	IT project completed without deficiency	IT project completed with minor deficiency	IT project completed with major deficiency	IT project was canceled or put on hold
From the perspective of the project manager	☐	☐	☐	☐
From the perspective of the project sponsor	☐	☐	☐	☐
From the perspective of the end user	☐	☐	☐	☐

The next set of questions will assess if you used one or more specific project risk management tools or techniques for the IT project you selected.

For the IT project you selected, please respond if you used one or more of the following tools or techniques within the Plan Risk Management process.

18. Indicate if you used one or more of the following tools or techniques in your IT project.

	Yes	No
Defined risk variance thresholds	☐	☐
Defined risk impact and probability scales	☐	☐
Defined risk escalation roles and responsibilities	☐	☐
Defined risk management review procedures	☐	☐
Defined risk communication and reporting	☐	☐
Defined risk prioritization as linked to project objectives	☐	☐
Defined risk templates or documents	☐	☐
Defined risk in the form of a cause and effect	☐	☐

For the IT project you selected, please respond if you used one or more of the following tools or techniques within the Identify Risks process.

19. Indicate if you used one or more of the following tools or techniques in your IT project.

	Yes	No
Identified risks as related to project assumptions and constraints	☐	☐
Identified risks through brainstorming	☐	☐
Identified risks through expert review	☐	☐
Identified risks through cause-and-effect relationship	☐	☐
Identified risks by using checklists or historical documents	☐	☐
Identified risks through use of prompt lists or questionnaire	☐	☐
Identified risks through work breakdown structure review	☐	☐
Identified risks through strengths, weaknesses, opportunities or threats analysis	☐	☐

For the IT project you selected, please respond if you used one or more of the following tools or techniques within the Perform Qualitative Risk Analysis process.

20. Indicate if you used one or more of the following tools or techniques in your IT project.

	Yes	No
Estimated probability (for example, low, medium or high) of identified risks occurring	☐	☐
Estimated impact (for example, low, medium or high) to project if identified risks occurred	☐	☐

	Yes	No
Used probability and impact scores to rank risks	☐	☐
Identified top project risks or opportunities as related to one another	☐	☐

For the IT project you selected, please respond if you used one or more of the following tools or techniques within the Perform Quantitative Risk Analysis process.

21. Indicate if you used one or more of the following tools or techniques in your IT project.

	Yes	No
Calculated risk through use of Decision Tree Analysis	☐	☐
Calculated risk through use of Monte Carlo simulation	☐	☐
Calculated risk through use of Expected Monetary Value (EMV)	☐	☐
Calculated total project sensitivity to risk	☐	☐
Calculated total overall project risk	☐	☐
Calculated total project confidence to achieve stated goals	☐	☐
Identified top project risks or opportunities as related to project objectives	☐	☐

For the IT project you selected, please respond if you used one or more of the following tools or techniques within the Plan Risk Responses process.

22. Indicate if you used one or more of the following tools or techniques in your IT project.

	Yes	No
Responded to identified risks by modifying the project plan	☐	☐
Responded to identified risks through contingency planning or use of reserve	☐	☐
Responded to identified risks through mitigation planning	☐	☐
Responded to identified risks through predetermined "if-then" structure	☐	☐
Responded to identified risks by assigning risk ownership	☐	☐
Responded to identified risks through contract agreement with stakeholders	☐	☐

For the IT project you selected, please respond if you used one or more of the following tools or techniques within the Monitor and Control Risks process.

23. Indicate if you used one or more of the following tools or techniques in your IT project.

	Yes	No
Performed reserve analysis to track or spend contingency funds used for risks as they occurred	☐	☐
Performed risk audits for assessment and compliance to chosen risk management approach	☐	☐
Performed risk reassessment reviews to	☐	☐

	Yes	No
ensure risk register remained up-to-date		
Performed variance analysis to compare forecast and actual risk impacts	☐	☐
Performed trend analysis to assess the effectiveness of risk responses	☐	☐
Performed risk reassessment activity	☐	☐
Held status meetings to review active, occurred or retired risks	☐	☐

INDEX

CURRICULUM VITAE

SETH J. GILLESPIE, PH.D.
MBA, PMP, PMI-ACP, CSM, ITIL, CISSP

linkedin.com/in/sethgillespie

STATEMENT OF TEACHING PHILOSOPHY

As someone who has had a successful professional career and a vast dedication to lifelong learning, I now strive to be the best educator I can be to give back to society and to pass along knowledge so others can better themselves. Seeing people advance in their careers and live to their highest potential is motivating to me and a driving force behind my desire to teach. I believe education has the power to transform a person's life – both in the short- and long-term. My passion is the constant pursuit and sharing of the latest thinking and understanding of our world and human society, especially as applied to organizations. We need programs and policies that embrace change, and encourage people, to bring their dedication and creativity to work. My goal is to help students to develop an awareness of what makes successful organizations by developing their critical thinking skills, through learning about stimulating new ways to view the world. I get most excited seeing students have those 'light bulb' moments when they understand a new idea and can talk about its positive impact in their world.

To me, the most important skill for an instructor is listening. We must listen to our students to understand where they are so we can meet them at their level and learning style with the curriculum. In so doing, we learn much about them, ourselves, and the subject matter, too. I believe the best teachers are facilitators, rather than lecturers, guiding critical discourse and drawing out a student's best, so they may apply what they learned in class to their lives in a meaningful way. I strive to create a safe environment where students feel free to actively participate, not just passively learn. I prefer a student-centered approach to engaging students in activities to allow them to practice new skills and visualize how the frameworks open up possibilities for new actions. I evaluate their progress through collaborative research projects, research papers, presentations, and answers to discussion questions. This approach creates transformational learning, and it is critical to developing new competencies and demands a focus on critical thinking and academic rigor.

Students should be given the opportunity to challenge themselves to reach their higher potential through measured, competency-based educational standards. In earning credentials, students should be given the tools, resources, and necessary instruction to achieve goals within an environment that facilities innovation and decisive collaboration. To foster an effective learning environment, I engage with students frequently, adding additional value and perspective to drive interest. Ultimately, students deserve to be respected, treated fairly and held accountable in a transparent process throughout their journey.

EXPERIENCE SUMMARY

- 20+ years, Data Center Management (Fortune 500)
- 17+ years, IT Project Management
- 15+ years, Project, Portfolio and Program Management
- 10+ years, IT Staff Management (Private, Public)
- 4+ years, System Engineer

PERSONAL AND PROFESSIONAL ATTRIBUTES

- Seasoned professional with 20+ years of valuable experience in the field of Information Technology and Management within diverse industries such as Hardware and Software Engineering, Pharmaceuticals and Biotech, Motion Picture Films, Natural and Renewable Energy

Generation, and Management Consulting.
- Adapt in multi-cultural environments with significant time leading diverse teams in Germany, Italy, Singapore and China, as well as multiple sites within the United States
- Efficiently and creatively uses experience to identify ways students can learn and discuss material in courses
- Applies various teaching styles and adapts instruction to students with diverse learning styles
- Excels in demanding, outcome-oriented, and dynamic work environments
- Proven teaching strategies that promotes student(s) success
- Effective collaborator leading high-performing teams by fostering relationships and scope ownership responsibilities

INDUSTRY TEACHING & TRAINING EXPERIENCE

Industry Educator

Teacher and trainer of industry courses in Project Management and Information Technology courses.

2010 – Present, Sr. Project Manager
Apple Inc., Cupertino, CA

Courses Taught:
- Categories of Impact
- Effective Communication
- Impactful and Effective Writing

2008 – 2010, Sr. Project Manager
Chevron, San Ramon, CA

Courses Taught:
- Project Management: Critical Path Analysis for Project Server
- Advanced Topics: Task Drivers and Master Projects, and Project Client-Server Administration

2006 – 2008, Sr. Project Manager
Siemens, Newark, CA

Courses Taught:
- Microsoft Project Server: Basics, Advanced, and Executive Reporting
- Project Manager: Best Practices

2001 – 2005, Project Manager
Chiron, Emeryville, CA

Courses Taught:
- 21-CFR Part 11: Electronic Document Record Keeping Requirements
- Desktop Training for Document Management: Hands-on Lab

1997 – 2001, Systems Engineer
Pfizer, La Jolla, CA

Courses Taught:
- Documentum 101: End Customer Scenarios
- Train-the-Trainer: Advanced Topics
- Content Management Best Practices: Beginner, Intermediate, and Advanced
- Client-Server Basics: Hands-on Lab

PROFESSIONAL POSITIONS IN ACADEMIA

2016, Exam Writer
Project Management Institute (PMI)

- Certified writer for exams applying knowledge and subject matter expertise.

2001, 2002, 2003, Subject Matter Expert
Computing Technology Industry Association (CompTIA)

- Subject Matter Expert and Exam writer for CDIA+, E-Biz+, IT Project+, A+ Hardware and Software.

BUSINESS EXPERIENCE PORTFOLIO

01/10 – present, Sr. Project Manager / Program Manager
Apple, Cupertino, CA

- Manage / oversight of personnel / work schedules for hundreds of personnel including: operations, networking, systems engineers, capacity manager, and database engineers), with direct reports of program management for >100s of applications / system deployments for US-based (CA, NV, OR, NC) and worldwide sites; management of budgets of >$25M (per program)
- Design / structure architecture of physical Data Center security for Apple Pay (including intrusion detection) for four world-wide, data centers (Maiden, NC; Prineville OR; Shanghai and Beijing, China); validated access controls to high security areas for site(s) per legal / contractual requirements including: network / computer-related purchases; systems quality assurance (QA) included: production, test, development, certification, performance validation, live data storage, simulation(s), disaster recovery, and penetration testing; resulting in on-time and on-budget construction and deliverables
- Organized migration of 2,000+ systems of 34 groups and six lines of business for IT services including: 2+ petabytes of storage (single data center in Newark, CA) to two target data centers (Reno, NV; Maiden, NC), including build-out of core data center services and infrastructure (Network, DNS, NTP, Backup Systems / Compute(s) prior to migration(s); results were complete / error free migration from source to target locations with high integrity and minimal downtime

- Designed / managed deployment of fault-tolerant, high-availability Network and Compute architecture supporting >1 billion aggregated user-authentication requests, including design, procurement, and installation of 40 distributed and discrete PODs comprised of Network and Compute clusters within four data centers in active-active mode; tested simulated traffic to demonstrate capability to exceed 10x normal load for internal and external identity management functions, including holiday sales traffic historically for four years
- Developed solution that aggregated global log files for business metrics used to diagnose at risk systems, isolate / resolve system technical issues
- Worked with internal business groups to develop, design, and deploy cloud-based, anti-fraud, management system with artificial intelligence (AI)-machine learning and commodity based server nodes, resulting in cost savings from reduced fraud; innovated a cost effective way to centralize versus distribute processing load resulting in scalable systems
- Coordinated >20+ different internal IT groups and business units to form a master, disaster recovery plan visible at the C-level, including team feedback, documentation, simulation of results, ratification, and periodic updates, resulting in C-suite approval of plan managing multiple staff organization-wide to increase disaster recovery efforts by >75%, and adding policy strategy for process improvement and ongoing testing

05/08 – 01/10, Sr. Project Manager / IT Portfolio Manager Chevron, San Ramon, CA

- Managed staff responsible for System and Database Engineering within the project management support program offering 100% uptime for client-server based enterprise project management software, utilized by thousands of project managers worldwide
- Provided management of multi-disciplinary Microsoft Server based IT programs, including Database and Internet Applications, resulting in high-quality, on-

schedule, on-budget results

- Performed audit(s), reduced IT hardware footprint in Data Center by consolidating infrastructure via use of server virtualization, space savings, and reduction of power costs and eliminating redundant IT software licenses resulting in cost savings of >$100K, re-invested savings into server upgrades for capacity management
- Managed uptime objectives through server vitalization, unit testing, and validation prior to code and software updates, minimizing impact to both client and server-based software packages

10/06 – 03/08, Sr. Project Manager / Technical Manager
Siemens, Newark, CA

- Managed personnel including: system engineers, network engineers, site services and change management performing patch management, production launches, data center troubleshooting
- Responsible Production Data Center program management for California (from Newark site); coordinated and liaised with California state government reps for services: managed hundreds of servers during full lifecycle, including purchasing, deployment and retirement; results were significate cost savings through hardware consolation and 25% increased allocation efficiency of servers, including savings via reduction in overhead costs
- Created data center process improvement and strategic IT upgrades to critical Microsoft-Server based 24x7 systems (customized Microsoft Project Server implementation) with zero downtime, optimizing resource prioritization, increasing system engineer productivity by 20% and program portfolio management efficiency by 40%; implemented centralized time / project tracking system to compare / forecast work-hours at task level; reports with metrics guided/aligned management improvements of data center strategy; resulting in ~$250K in client savings in first year
- Liaised with information security in re-architecture of

159

database, application and web services by creating dedicated operational zones, resulting in improved security and network segmentation

08/05 – 04/06, Project Manager / Staffing Manager
Dell, Round Rock, TX

- Managed staff of >100 IT contract workers for California-based clients including full-cycle recruiting, hiring, retention, and performance evaluations for managed services, including unexpected demand for increased staff by 2.5x for last-minute contract for client, resulting in meeting contract deliverables for hardware and software deployment
- Reduced number of product SKUs by 50% simplifying the ordering process for client and increasing revenue for company by $1M over a 30-day period

04/05 – 07/05, Project Manager / Data Center Migrations
Lucasfilm, San Rafael, CA

- Created and directed master program and staff schedule for two Data Center migrations, enabling strategic visibility / accountability for management and staff to reduce program delays
- Oversight included System Engineers, Desktop Engineers, and Onsite Construction and Patch Plan management, resulting in zero defects subsequent to move and bringing facility on board
- Responsible for on-schedule and on-budget relocation for new, purpose-built company data center and IT systems, including Starwars.com, from San Rafael, CA to new data center in The Presidio of San Francisco, CA; management included a risk management plan for migration, resulting in risk avoidance

06/01 – 04/05, Project Manager / Worldwide Deployments
Chiron, Emeryville, CA

- Supervised data center staff (including physical presence

for oversight in Italy/Germany) worldwide to deploy database, application, web servers and software in Emeryville, CA, Seattle, WA, Marburg, Germany and Siena, Italy
- Spearheaded remediation of electronic FDA mandated records keeping requirements mandated by FDA for IT regulatory compliance for record-keeping of 25 business systems and 15 software packages company-wide, with deliverables on-time and on-budget, aiding business continuity

08/97 – 05/01, Systems Engineer / IT Portfolio Manager
Pfizer, La Jolla, CA

- Technical lead manager for build-out / deployment for data center including, physical site selection, racking, powering, cabling and relocation of existing data center services with minimal downtime and impact to research and development (R&D) scientists
- Managed IT portfolio of hardware and software procurement, installation, and maintenance for 500 employees at four physical sites within San Diego County with an annual budget of ~$1.5M

ENTREPRENEURIAL EXPERIENCE

2008 – Present, Founder and President
Looking Up to You, LLC

- Charity work, non-profit support and mentoring services

2004 – 2010, CEO and President
John316Management, Inc.

- Professional-services and management consulting

FORMAL EDUCATION

- 2014, Doctor of Philosophy (Ph.D.), Organization and Management, Capella University, Minneapolis, MN
- 2004, Master of Business Administration, Technology Management, University of Phoenix, Phoenix, AZ
- 1997, Bachelor of Science, Molecular Biology, University of California, San Diego, CA

CAREER TRAINING, PROFESSIONAL CERTIFICATIONS & TECHNICAL TRAINING

- 2016 – 2019, Certified Information Systems Security Professional (CISSP), (ISC)², License # 573231
- 2015 - 2017, Certified ScrumMaster (CSM), Cert # 000449272 Scrum Alliance, Indianapolis, IN
- 2005 - 2021, Project Management Professional (PMP), Cert #215557, PMI, Newtown Square, PA
- 2015 - 2021, Agile Certified Practitioner (PMI-ACP; 21 hours), Cert #1850873, PMI, Newtown Square, PA
- 2016, (ISC)² Information Systems Security (ISC)², Professional Training (40 hours)
- 2012, IT Infrastructure Library (ITIL v3), Cert #GR750030946SG, AXELOS, London, UK
- 2012, Information Technology Infrastructure Library (ITIL) v3, License # GR750030946SG
- 2005 – 2021, Project Management Institute (PMI)
- 2002, CDIA+ Certification, License # COMP10229208
- 2003, IT Project+, Cert #COMP10229208, CompTIA, Downers Grove, IL
- 2003, IT Project+ Certification, License # COMP10229208
- 2002, Manager, Prepaid Legal Services Certification (Legal Shield)
- 2002, Director, Prepaid Legal Services Certification (Legal Shield)
- 2002, Fast Start to Success, Prepaid Legal Services Certification (Legal Shield)

- 2002, Toastmaster International Communication and Leadership Program (Competent Toastmaster)
- 2002, Specialized Certificate in Microsoft Database Administration (200 hours), University of California, San Diego, CA
- 2001, Formulating Business Strategy, Stanford University, Palo Alto, CA
- 2001, Building a Vision for Yourself or Your Organization, Stanford University, Palo Alto, CA
- 2000, A+ Hardware and Software Certification, License # E3CDTT0506
- 2005 - 2021, PMP (Project Management Professional), License # 215557
- 1999, Microsoft Certified Professional (MCP), License # A553-5979, University of California, San Diego, CA
- 2016 - 2019, Certified Information System Security Professional (CISSP), ISC^2, Clearwater, Florida
- 2003, Computing Technology Industry Association (CompTIA), E-Biz+ Certification, License # COMP10229208
- 2002, Quality Management (30 hours), University of California, Berkeley, CA
- 2002, Project Risk Management (30 hours), University of California, Berkeley, CA
- 2002, Project Planning and Control (30 hours), University of California, Berkeley, CA
- 2002, Managing without Authority (32 hours), Stanford University, CA
- 2001. Formulating Business Strategy (8 hours), Stanford University, CA
- 2001, XML (24 hours), University of California, San Diego, CA
- 2001, Software Project Management (34 hours), University of California, Berkeley, CA
- 2001, Project Management (34 hours), University of California, Berkeley, CA
- 2001, Human Factors and Team Dynamics (40 hours), University of California, Berkeley, CA
- 2001, Building a Vision for Yourself or Your Organization

(8 hours), Stanford University, CA
- 2000, Specialized Certificate in Computer Networks (120 hours), University of California, San Diego, CA
- 2000, UNIX Systems Security (24 hours), University of California, San Diego, CA
- 2000, UNIX Systems Administration (24 hours), University of California, San Diego, CA
- 2000, Oracle: SQL and PL/SQL (32 hours), University of California, San Diego, CA
- 2000, Microsoft Systems Engineering (145 hours), UC San Diego, La Jolla, CA
- 2000, Microsoft SQL Database Design (80 hours), University of California, San Diego, CA
- 2000, Microsoft Database Administration (200 hours), UC San Diego, La Jolla, CA
- 2000, Managing Multiple Projects, Objectives and Deadlines (8 hours), SkillPath Seminars
- 2000, How to Become a Better Communicator (8 hours), SkillPath Seminars
- 1999, UNIX Operating Systems (24 hours), University of California, San Diego, CA
- 1999, Microsoft Internet Systems (145 hours), UC San Diego, La Jolla, CA
- 1999, Business Writing for Professionals (8 hours), SkillPath Seminars
- 1999, Specialized Certificate in Microsoft Systems Engineering (145 hours), University of California, San Diego, CA
- 1999, Specialized Certificate in Microsoft Internet Systems (145 hours), University of California, San Diego, CA
- 1999, Microsoft Certified Professional (MCP), Cert #1525112, Microsoft, Redmond, WA

MEMBERSHIPS AND AFFILIATIONS

- 2016 – present, Member, International Information System Security Certification Consortium (ISC)²
- 2001- present, Member, Project Management Institute

- 2008 – 2009, Vice President, Microsoft Project User Group (MPUG), Vice President
- 2003, Committee Member, Liquent CoreAlliance Program, Committee Member
- 2002 – 2003, President, LiveLink West Coast User Group (LWCUG), President
- 2002 – 2003, Member, Institute of Electrical and Electronic Engineers (IEEE)
- 2000 – 2003, Member, Computing Technology Industry Association (CompTIA)
- 2000 – 2003, Group Chair, CoreDossier West Coast User Group (CWCUG)
- 2000 – 2003, Vice President, Documentum West Coast User Group (WCDUG)

COMMUNITY SERVICE AND LEADERSHIP

- 2015 – present, City Team: Adult Rehabilitation and Outreach, teaching job skills to at-risk adult students,
- San Jose, CA
- 2011, Cambodia Children Rescue: Lab instructor and facilitator, including analytical skill development, Phnom Penh, Cambodia
- 2009, Little Lambs: Mentored and provided life-skills to over 100 students nearing graduation, Kiev, Ukraine
- 2006, Park Avenue District Committee: Chaired $5M urban improvement program, Emeryville, CA

PROFESSIONAL AND SCHOLARLY PRESENTATIONS

- 11/09, The Value of Project Management when Budgets are Tight, Microsoft Project User Group (MPUG), San Francisco, CA
- 12/08, Microsoft Project Server Admin Tips and Tricks, San Francisco, CA
- 09/07, Advanced Project Management Training, Siemens, IT Solutions and Services Newark, CA
- 03/03, Working with Virtual Teams, LiveLink West Coast

User Group (LWCUG), San Francisco, CA
- 08/03, Managing a Global Rollout, Liquent CoreAlliance, Miami, FL
- 08/03, User Group Community "Back to Basics", Miami, FL
- 03/03, Lessons Learned, Documentum West Coast User Group (DWCUG), San Francisco, CA
- 11/02, CoreDossier Expansion Project, CoreDossier West Coast User Group (CWCUG), Emeryville, CA
- 11/02, Technical Aspects of Migration and Validation, New Orleans, LA
- 02/02, Getting Started with Documentum, La Jolla, CA

CONFERENCES ATTENDED

- Winter 2014, Edward Tufte: Presenting Data and Information, Santa Clara, CA
- Winter 2007, Microsoft Project Conference, Seattle, WA
- Fall 2005, Special Interest Group on Computer Graphics and Interactive Techniques (Siggraph), Los Angeles, CA
- Fall 2004, Electronics Expo (E3), Los Angeles, CA
- Summer 2003, Microsoft Windows Launch, San Francisco, CA
- Summer 2003, Liquent CoreAlliance, Miami, FL
- Summer 2002, Liquent CoreAlliance, New Orleans, LA
- Summer 2002, Electronic Submissions (eSub) Conference,
- Washington D.C.
- Summer 2001, Microsoft Certified Professional (MCP) TechMentor Conference, Orlando, FL
- Summer 2001, ProjectWorld Conference, San Jose, CA
- Summer 2001, Documentum Momentum Conference, Chicago, IL
- Summer 2000, International Academy of Human Rights (IAOA), Strasbourg, France
- Summer 1999, Computer Dealers Exhibition (COMDEX),
- Chicago, IL
- Summer 1999, Windows World Expo, Chicago, IL

RESIDENCIES AND COLLOQUIA

- Winter 2007, Ph.D. Colloquium Track I, Capella University
- Fall 2007, Ph.D. Colloquium Track II, Capella University
- Fall 2008, Ph.D. Colloquium Track III, Capella University

ARTICLES AND RESEARCH

Gillespie, S. (2014). Correlational Study of Risk Management and Information Technology Project Success. Capella University, Minneapolis, MN.

Gillespie, S. (2009, November). Value of Project Management when Budgets are Tight. Slideshare.

Gillespie, S. (2009, November). The Mentor Loop. Slideshare.

Gillespie, S. (2009, November). Managing Without Authority: A Stanford University Prospective. Slideshare.

Gillespie, S. (2009, November). GTD Founder David Allen: Lessons Learned. Slideshare.

Gillespie, S. (2009, July). Post-Chernobyl Ukraine, an Orphanage Perspective. Slideshare.

Gillespie, S. (2008, March). Project Management Portfolio. Slideshare.

ARTICLES CITED IN

Duvall, M. (2002, October). Documentation: From Out of Step to Tried and True. Baseline.

Liquent. (2003, July). Case Study: Migration and Validation: A Successful Team Effort Between Chiron and Liquent.

Workshare. (2003, June). Case Study: Chiron Corporation and Workshare Synergy.

AWARDS, GRANTS AND HONORS

- 2014, Capella University, Graduate with Distinction
- 2012, iPhone Product Launch: Key Contributor, Apple Inc.
- 2011, Outstanding Teamwork with R&D Applications
- 2010, Recipient, Dr. Harold Kerzner Award

- 2009, Chevron, Execute with Excellence
- 2007, Siemens, Employee Recognition Award
- 2002, CompTIA, Certificate of Appreciation A+ Certification Program

SUBJECT MATTER EXPERTISE

- Data Center Operations: Rack, Power, Cable, Monitoring and Patch Plan Management
- Database Engineering: Oracle, TimesTen (x10), MySQL, Cassandra, Hadoop, CouchBase and Mongo
- Network Engineering: DC Core, Gateway, Switch, Firewall, WAF, VPN, and Load Balancing
- Procurement: Bill of Materials, Purchase Requisition, Approval, Delivery, and Receipt
- Project, Program and Portfolio Management: Local, Global and Internet-Scale Infrastructure
- Security: PCI, PII, SOX Compliance, including Tiered Architecture (Web, App, Database)
- Systems Engineering: iOS, Linux, Solaris, AIX, NAS/SAN/RAID/JBOD and Virtualized
- Machine Learning / Disaster Recovery / Asset Recovery

LEARNING MANAGEMENT SYSTEMS

- WebCT
- Udemy
- OpenEdx
- Moodle
- Lynda
- Blackboard

ADDITIONAL SUBJECT MATTER EXPERTISE

- Human Relations
- Information Technology
- International Business
- Management
- Management Consulting
- Managerial Communication
- Managerial Finance
- Managing People
- Marketing Management
- Operations Management
- Organizational Behavior
- Organizational Theory
- Project Management
- Research Methods
- Risk Management
- Technology Management

BOOKS PUBLISHED

Gillespie, S. (2016). *Correlational Study of Risk Management and Information Technology Project Success: A Must Read for IT Managers and Project Stakeholders* [Print Version]. Virginia Beach, VA: DBC Publishing. http://amzn.to/2b6X8j7

Gillespie, S. (2016) *Cultural Change Sarbanes-Oxley and Information Technology* [Kindle Version]. Virginia Beach, VA: DBC Publishing. http://amzn.to/2b8TiVp

Gillespie, S. (2016) *Risk Management: An Enterprise Dilemma* [Kindle Version]. Virginia Beach, VA: DBC Publishing. http://amzn.to/2bmd28o

Gillespie, S. (2016) *Server Virtualization: A Cost Savings Strategy* [Kindle Version]. Virginia Beach, VA: DBC Publishing. http://amzn.to/2b6NhLv

ABOUT THE AUTHOR

Dr. Gillespie, originally from San Diego, CA is currently based out of Silicon Valley, located within the San Francisco Bay Area. In addition to being PMP®, PMI-ACP®, CSM®, ITIL® and CISSP® certified, he earned a Bachelor of Science in Molecular Biology, with a Minor in Economics, a Master of Business Administration (MBA) with an emphasis in Technology Management, and a Doctor of Philosophy (Ph.D.) in Organization and Management, specializing in Information Technology Management.

Gillespie is a popular speaker, lecturer and subject matter expert in the field of IT Management, Project Management, Risk Management, Organizational Management, and large-scale Information Technology infrastructure projects, programs and portfolios. In addition to speaking engagements, he has participated as a noted exam writer for numerous CompTIA and Project Management Institute (PMI) certifications.

In his free time, Gillespie enjoys traveling and assisting in social justice causes benefiting under-served groups worldwide.

ABOUT THE BOOK

A must read for project management professionals, managers and stakeholders who want to better understand what impacts IT project success the most in order to achieve more favorable project results. Since many IT projects fail to fully meet original goals, examination of project risk management tools and techniques will help to inform and educate the reader on important topics within this often misunderstood body of knowledge.

Few studies have examined the relationship between the use of project risk management processes and project success as measured by project outcomes, including budget, schedule and scope. Readers will, therefore, gain a competitive ability to understand current and relevant academic and non-academic research in the area of project risk management, gaps in the research, best practices that can be incorporated into their projects, programs or portfolios, as well as learning about recommendations for further research.

This book addresses the effectiveness of utilizing project risk management processes as they correlate to improved IT project success, based on a research study and survey of nearly 100 project management professionals. After reading this book, you will take away specific and concrete evidence that emphasizes which project risk management tools and techniques often correlate with project success, irrespective of a project manager's level of education, experience or type of certification.

Websites

Visit the Author's Website:
books.sethgillespie.com

Author's Blog:
blog.sethgillespie.com

LinkedIn Profile:
linkedin.com/in/sethgillespie

Follow on Twitter:
twitter.com/sg_phd

Books by Seth J. Gillespie, Ph.D.

Correlational Study of Risk Management
and Information Technology Project Success:
A Must Read for IT Managers and Project Stakeholders

Risk Management: An Enterprise Dilemma

Server Virtualization: A Cost Savings Strategy

Cultural Change: Sarbanes-Oxley and Information Technology

Correlational Study of Risk Management and Information Technology Project Success:
A Must Read for IT Managers and Project Stakeholders

amzn.to/2b6X8j7

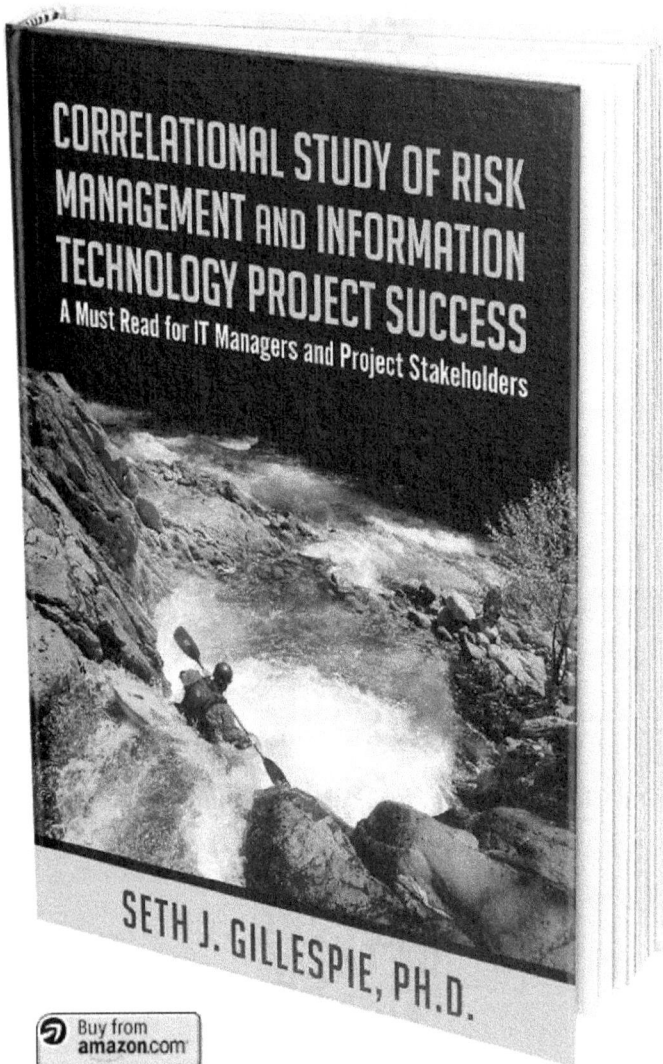

Risk Management:
An Enterprise Dilemma

amzn.to/2bmd28o

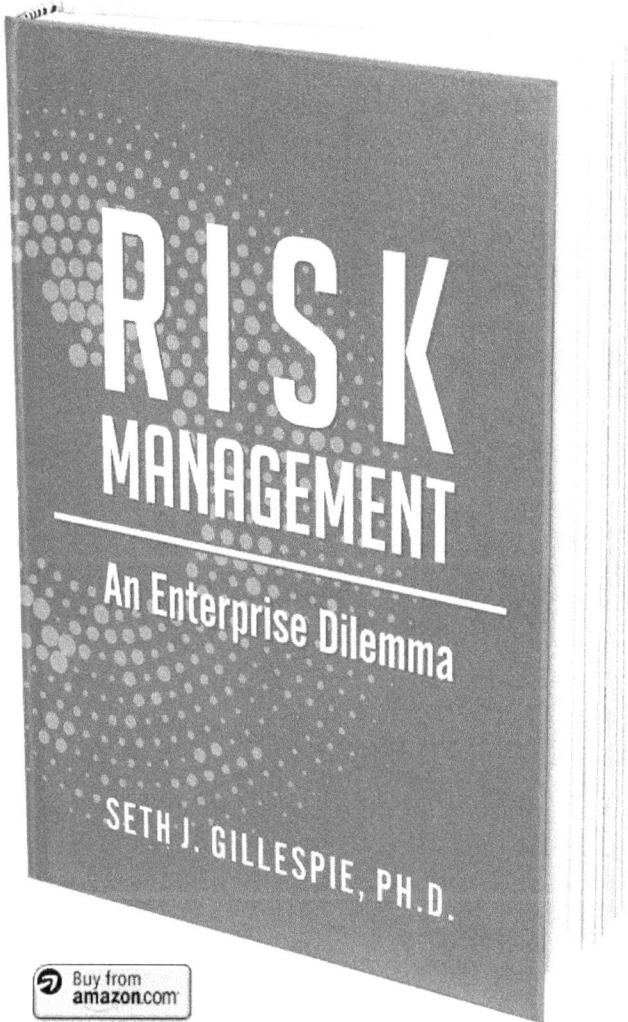

Server Virtualization:
A Cost Savings Strategy

amzn.to/2b6NhLv

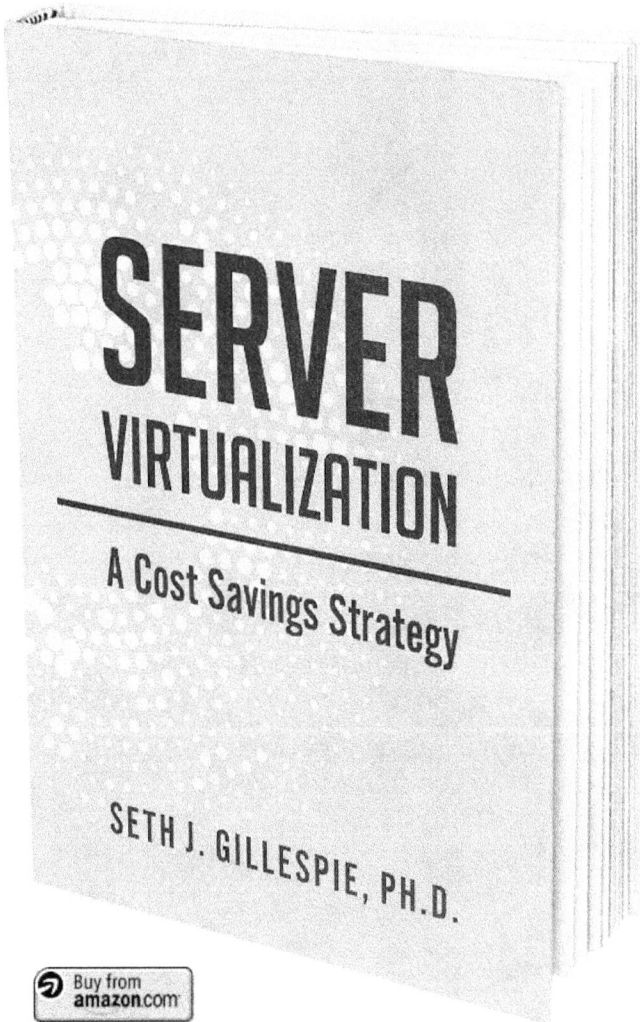

Cultural Change:
Sarbanes-Oxley and Information Technology

amzn.to/2b8TiVp

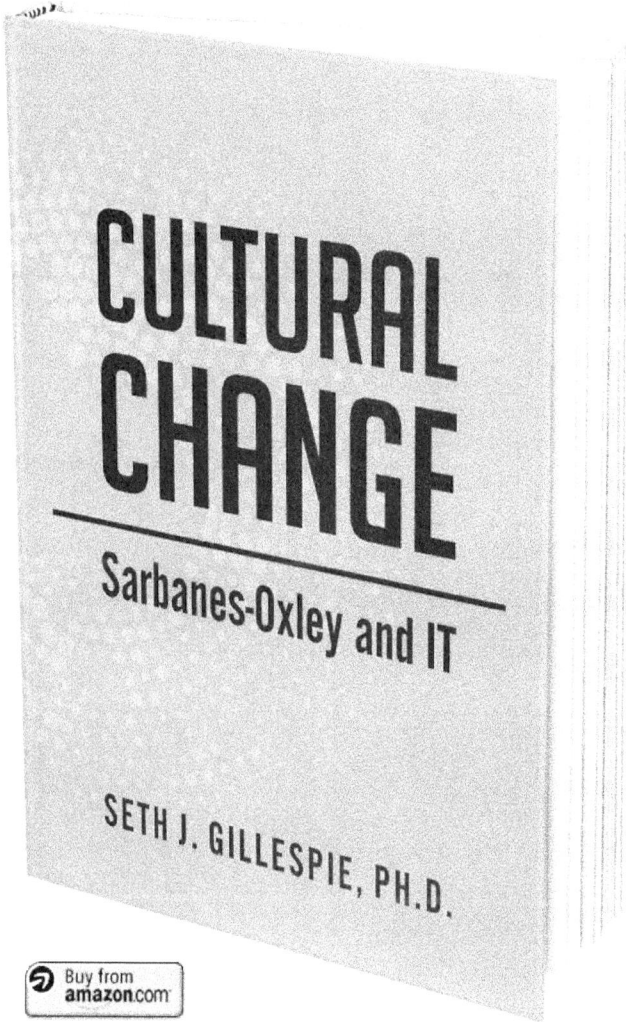

www.ingramcontent.com/pod-product-compliance
Lightning Source LLC
Chambersburg PA
CBHW050106210326
41519CB00015BA/3841